'As a "puffer nutter" I own numerous books development of railways. Selection of a particular gauge was often driven by geographic or engineering considerations. The many different Australian gauges have always been cause of much "head shaking".

Tim's book explores the solutions found in many countries and the irresistible move toward a standardised national Australian network culminating in the completion of the great north-south railway to Darwin.

This book is both highly educational and a damn good read.'

Sam Burgess OAM
Former chairman Zig Zag Railway and formerly of Qantas and British Airways

'A fascinating view of railways throughout the world by an Australian railway do-er. Tim is one of the few people who have combined an interest and expertise in railways into doing something worthwhile for his country.

Without his help, the Alice Springs to Darwin railway and other projects in Australia would simply never have happened.

A great read on railways around the world as seen from Down Under.'

Mike Mohan
Former US railroader, Southern Pacific Railways and now ARG, Perth

TRANSCONTINENTAL TRAIN ODYSSEY

THE GHAN, THE KHYBER, THE GLOBE

A portion of the royalties from this book will be shared equally between the Fred Hollows Foundation, Frontier Services, previously the Australian Inland Mission, and the Royal Flying Doctor Service of Australia.

TRANSCONTINENTAL TRAIN ODYSSEY
THE GHAN, THE KHYBER, THE GLOBE

TIM FISCHER

ALLEN&UNWIN

Verification:
The confirmation of research findings has involved using the comprehensive *Jane's World Railways* 44th Edition, with permission.

Cover photograph:
The Ghan on the Great Larapinta Grade just north of Alice Springs,
bound for Darwin for the first time, 2 February 2004. Photograph courtesy of
Barry Skipsey and GSR.

First published in 2004

Allen & Unwin
83 Alexander Street
Crows Nest NSW 2065
Australia
Phone: (61 2) 8425 0100
Fax: (61 2) 9906 2218
Email: info@allenandunwin.com
Web: www.allenandunwin.com

National Library of Australia
Cataloguing-in-Publication entry:

Fischer, Tim, 1946–.
Transcontinental train odyssey : the Ghan, the Khyber, the globe.

Bibliography.
Includes index
ISBN 1 74114 450 7.

1. Fischer, Tim, 1946–. 2. Railroads - History.
3. Railroad travel - Anecodotes. I. Title.

910.4

Typeset by Midland Typesetters, Maryborough
Printed by McPherson's Printing Group, Maryborough, Victoria

10 9 8 7 6 5 4 3 2

PART THREE: DARWIN AT LAST

PART FOUR: THE FUTURE

Dedication	To my wife Judy, sons Harrison and Dominic, and my late father Julius Ralph Fischer, who first introduced me to trains.
Inspiration	Those people who know, or want to know, what successful rail is all about.
Salutation	In salute of those many people, including engineers, surveyors, financiers, workers and project managers who over the years have helped or continue to help make rail happen.

'Now comes a singular thing: the oddest thing, the strangest thing, the most unaccountable marvel that Australia can show. At the frontier between New South Wales and Victoria our multitude of passengers were routed out of their snug beds by lantern light in the morning in the biting cold to change cars on a railroad that has no break in it from Sydney to Melbourne. Think of the paralysis of intellect that gave that idea birth; imagine the boulder it emerged from, on some petrified legislator's shoulders. It is a narrow gauge [sic] to the frontier and a broader gauge thence to Melbourne. One or two reasons are given for this curious state of things. One is that it represents the jealousy existing between the two colonies—the two most important colonies of Australasia. What the other is I have forgotten, it could be but another effort to explain the inexplicable.'

Mark Twain (pseudonym of Samuel Langhorne Clemens), American author (1835–1910), after passing by train through Albury Station, Australia, around 1895

PREFACE

FROM TWO PRIME MINISTERS

Gough Whitlam, Port Augusta Town Hall, Port Augusta, 11 April 1975

In no area of government is there a greater need for modernisation and reform than the railways. In no area have there been greater constitutional and administrative obstacles to reform. The railways are usually historically regarded as the great instrument for unifying a continent. It was transcontinentals that united the United States, united the Canadian provinces, and united the Soviet Union from the Baltic to the Pacific.

One would have thought that railways would be the great instrument for uniting Australia. It has not turned out that way, because our railways were started in the middle of the last century by the states and they are still run, with the exception of the ANR, by the states. This occurs in the Australian federal system only.

In West Germany the railways are run by the federal government. In Canada there are two great railway systems, one run by the Canadian government and the other by a nationwide international company. In the United States all the railway systems are co-ordinated by the Interstate Commerce Commission.

In Australia, far from uniting our country, the railway systems have been organised so as to disrupt the unification of the nation. They have been used to centralise our settlement, our commerce, in state capitals. There is, fortunately, a provision in the Constitution which enables the Commonwealth with the consent of the states to build or acquire railways. It was because the states of South Australia and Western Australia permitted the Commonwealth to build a railway, that we got the east–west railway. It is because of that provision that the Commonwealth, with the consent of the state of South Australia, is now acquiring the non-metropolitan railways in South Australia.

This will transform the railway scene in Australia, east and west and north and south. It will be a very significant system and it will be an immense reinforcement and multiplication of the things that can be done.

Tomorrow we embark upon the construction of the railway from Tarcoola to Alice Springs, the largest railway project Australia has undertaken since before the First World War and one which will make an immense difference to the people in the centre. It will make a great difference to the tourist industry, the cattle industry, the mining industry.

I have always found romance in the construction of railways. Railways were the distinguishing features of those industrial countries which were settling vast new areas. The United States, the old Tsarist Empire, Canada all did it. Australia had to wait to do it this century. A new railway has always carried with it an aura of romance, a spirit of pioneering. Nothing suggests more vividly the determination of a vigorous society to develop its resources and improve its communications.

Something was missing from our national life during the long years when the railways were allowed to decline. Men and families who had given a lifetime of service to the railways were encouraged to lose faith in the importance and future of a great industry. I hope and believe that we are seeing the rebirth of the railways in this continent, the beginning of a new era of growth and development.

You can be sure that my government will do its utmost to see the railways prosper and resume their rightful, their historic role as the basis of an efficient, modern and economical transport system.

It is appropriate to have this commemoration in Port Augusta where it all began, where it all passes. Prosperous and efficient railways are an efficient and essential condition of a prosperous and efficient nation.

John Howard, East Arm Wharf, Darwin, Northern Territory of Australia,
17 January 2004

This is a great moment in the history of Australia. It's not just a great moment, important though it is in the history and the development of the Northern Territory, fulfilling an aspiration of course that you've heard so much about, born almost 100 years ago; but to the entire nation this is a reminder of Australia at its best. What has been brought to fruition today reminds all of us that if we persist, if we work together, if we keep our gaze fixed on a goal, there is absolutely nothing that Australians working together cannot achieve.

It's one of those moments that brings together both the history of this country, but also a very clear-eyed understanding of our future. The history over 100 years of the various attempts to build this railway has been very well documented and the debates of almost 100 years ago have been trawled through in minute detail by my two parliamentary colleagues and many others as they've come from Adelaide to us here in Darwin. And it is steeped in history and in a way you can see it symbolically as conquering that last element of the tyranny of distance, as Geoffrey Blainey put it, that always afflicted Australia.

So it has got a lot to do with our history but it's also got very much to do with our future, because one of the great hopes of this railway is that it will further cement the role and the place of Darwin as a great port and a great bridge and a great link with the associations, economic and otherwise, that Australia has with the nations of Asia and it is therefore in that way very much part of our future and very much bound up with the links between Australia and the nations of our region.

It is important on an occasion such as this to pay tribute to so many who've done so much to bring this about. I share the compliment paid by Rick Allert to Barry Coulter for the enormous energy that he displayed, his persistence dealing with people, the same people often in both government and opposition, at a federal level. I compliment the work of previous chief ministers of the Territory, and previous premiers of South Australia.

It was Dean Brown and Shane Stone who first came to me after I became prime minister to reinforce the joint support of the people of South Australia and the people of the Northern Territory for this project, and I compliment the current occupants of these two positions, Clare Martin and Mike Rann, on the persistence and commitment that both of them have displayed towards it. And may I say that I'm quietly very proud of the fact that I lead the national government that ultimately gave the decisive financial support at a federal level that made the project possible.

But the most important people in building the railway were those who constructed it and those who conceived it, the private sector people who organised the finance, and I pay particular tribute to Malcolm Kinnaird and Rick Allert, the two businessmen with which I've had the most association in the course of putting the railway together, to David Lesar, but finally and most importantly to the men and women of the Territory and other parts of Australia who worked on the railway, who finished it ahead of time, who finished it efficiently and made it what it is and that is a great tribute to Australian engineering skill and a great tribute to the capacity of the Australian people to conquer any obstacle and clear any hurdle if we work together and commit our collective wills to those goals. It's been done in a record time and it's an enormous tribute and I just want to pay a special tribute to the builders, the people whose great technical skills had so much to do with it.

GREAT AUSTRALIAN RAILWAY GAUGES

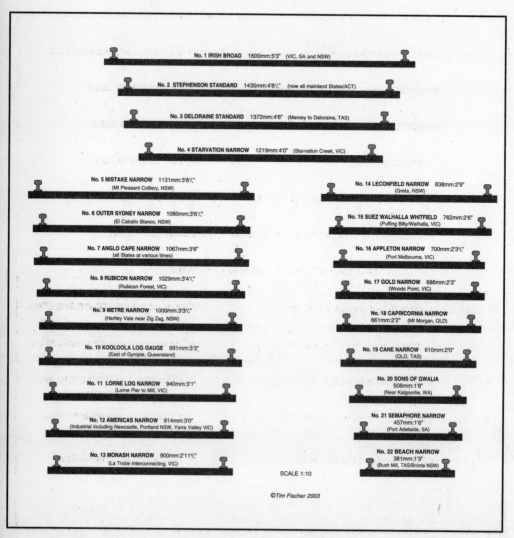

No. 1 IRISH BROAD   1600mm:5'3" (VIC, SA and NSW)

No. 2 STEPHENSON STANDARD   1435mm:4'8½" (now all mainland States/ACT)

No. 3 DELORAINE STANDARD   1372mm:4'6" (Mersey to Deloraine, TAS)

No. 4 STARVATION NARROW   1219mm:4'0" (Starvation Creek, VIC)

No. 5 MISTAKE NARROW   1131mm:3'8½"
(Mt Pleasant Colliery, NSW)

No. 14 LECONFIELD NARROW   838mm:2'9"
(Greta, NSW)

No. 6 OUTER SYDNEY NARROW   1080mm:3'6½"
(El Caballo Blanco, NSW)

No. 15 SUEZ WALHALLA WHITFIELD   762mm:2'6"
(Puffing Billy/Walhalla, VIC)

No. 7 ANGLO CAPE NARROW   1067mm:3'6"
(all States at various times)

No. 16 APPLETON NARROW   700mm:2'3½"
(Port Melbourne, VIC)

No. 8 RUBICON NARROW   1029mm:3'4½"
(Rubicon Forest, VIC)

No. 17 GOLD NARROW   686mm:2'3"
(Woods Point, VIC)

No. 9 METRE NARROW   1000mm:3'3½"
(Hartley Vale near Zig Zag, NSW)

No. 18 CAPRICORNIA NARROW
661mm:2'2"   (Mt Morgan, QLD)

No. 10 KOOLOOLA LOG GAUGE   991mm:3'3"
(East of Gympie, Queensland)

No. 19 CANE NARROW   610mm:2'0"
(QLD, TAS)

No. 11 LORNE LOG NARROW   940mm:3'1"
(Lorne Pier to Mill, VIC)

No. 20 SONS OF GWALIA
508mm:1'8"
(Near Kalgoorlie, WA)

No. 12 AMERICAS NARROW   914mm:3'0"
(Industrial including Newcastle, Portland NSW, Yarra Valley VIC)

No. 21 SEMAPHORE NARROW
457mm:1'6"
(Port Adelaide, SA)

No. 13 MONASH NARROW   900mm:2'11½"
(La Trobe Interconnecting, VIC)

No. 22 BEACH NARROW
381mm:1'3"
(Bush Mill, TAS/Bronte NSW)

SCALE 1:10

©Tim Fischer 2003

The gauges listed above reflect measurement of inside rail to inside rail and have been determined from railways that have operated or are operating 1 mile (1.6 kilometres) or more in Australia since 1831 when the Australian Agricultural Company built Australia's first railway in Newcastle, NSW, to export coal. Only Anglo Cape narrow gauge operates in all states, Stephenson standard gauge operates in all mainland states and from Adelaide to Darwin with FreighLink and the Ghan.

GREAT WORLD RAILWAY GAUGES

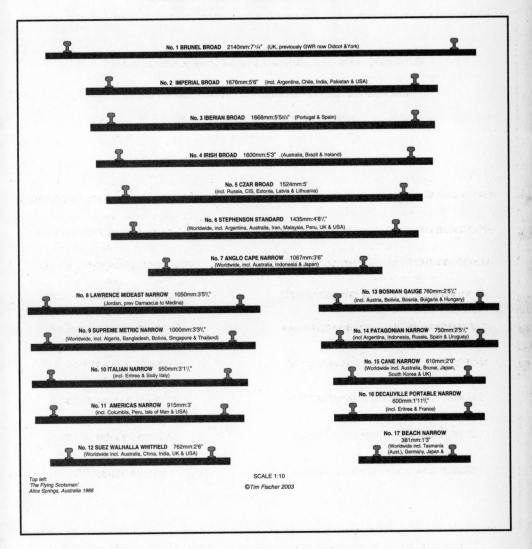

No. 1 BRUNEL BROAD   2140mm:7'1/4"   (UK, previously GWR now Didcot & York)

No. 2 IMPERIAL BROAD   1676mm:5'6"   (incl. Argentina, Chile, India, Pakistan & USA)

No. 3 IBERIAN BROAD   1668mm:5'52/3"   (Portugal & Spain)

No. 4 IRISH BROAD   1600mm:5'3"   (Australia, Brazil & Ireland)

No. 5 CZAR BROAD   1524mm:5'
(incl. Russia, CIS, Estonia, Latvia & Lithuania)

No. 6 STEPHENSON STANDARD   1435mm:4'81/2"
(Worldwide, incl. Argentina, Australia, Iran, Malaysia, Peru, UK & USA)

No. 7 ANGLO CAPE NARROW   1067mm:3'6"
(Worldwide, incl. Australia, Indonesia & Japan)

No. 8 LAWRENCE MIDEAST NARROW   1050mm:3'51/4"
(Jordan, prev Damascus to Medina)

No. 9 SUPREME METRIC NARROW   1000mm:3'33/8"
(Worldwide, incl. Algeria, Bangladesh, Bolivia, Singapore & Thailand)

No. 10 ITALIAN NARROW   950mm:3'11/4"
(incl. Eritrea & Sicily Italy)

No. 11 AMERICAS NARROW   915mm:3'
(incl. Columbia, Peru, Isle of Man & USA)

No. 12 SUEZ WALHALLA WHITFIELD   762mm:2'6"
(Worldwide incl. Australia, China, India, UK & USA)

No. 13 BOSNIAN GAUGE 760mm:2'51/2"
(incl. Austria, Bolivia, Bosnia, Bulgaria & Hungary)

No. 14 PATAGONIAN NARROW   750mm:2'51/2"
(incl Argentina, Indonesia, Russia, Spain & Uruguay)

No. 15 CANE NARROW   610mm:2'0"
(Worldwide incl. Australia, Brunei, Japan,
South Korea & UK)

No. 16 DECAUVILLE PORTABLE NARROW
600mm:1'11/5/"
(incl. Eritrea & France)

No. 17 BEACH NARROW
381mm:1'3"
(Worldwide incl. Tasmania
(Aust.), Germany, Japan &

Top left:
'The Flying Scotsman'
Alice Springs, Australia 1988

SCALE 1:10
©Tim Fischer 2003

These gauges and their nomenclature have been selected by the author. Measurement has been taken from inside rail to inside rail. Research involved inspection of rails in sixty countries and help from many individuals including Dmitry Zinoviev, John Birchmeier, Alex Grunbach, Owen Johnstone-Donnet, Dr Rob Lee, Scott Martin and Gerry Willis. Verification was supplied from Jane's comprehensive *44th World Railways*, with permission.

INTRODUCTION

CHAPTER ONE

THE RAILWAY REALMS

If the 19th century saw the birth of the railway, the 20th century saw its near death with the advent of the motor vehicle and the aeroplane. Now the 21st century is seeing railways bounce back, building on efficiencies and modernisation, high-speed train technology and unit freight train operations where trains are used for one freight purpose only, such as coal or containers.

The railways are back in business in a big way and this time around they are here to stay, even allowing for the ugly saga of terrorism and the odd spectacular financial failure from time to time.

There is no doubt the 'great rail recovery of the 21st century' has arrived, spearheaded by better government policies and priorities, along with important new projects. In the southern hemisphere it is the world's newest and smoothest transcontinental railway, standard gauge from Adelaide to Darwin, south–north across Australia. In the northern hemisphere it is the long overdue project to provide a true high-speed link from the Euro Tunnel near Folkestone through to St Pancras, London, and the first fully operational magnetic track that requires no wheels, the Maglev train from Shanghai to Pudong International Airport.

The birth of my interest in railways began many years ago, not with a model electric train set, as I never ever had one when growing up, although I did have a small wind-up Hornby set. (I eventually purchased a model electric train set, but it was only after I became a cabinet minister and, of course, it was for the kids!) My interest sprang from Monday night trips to the local rail station when I was a kid.

I recall the family discussions as to whether or not it was worth-while using scarce and costly petrol to drive the five kilometres into Boree Creek to meet the railmotor as it rolled down the Riverina branch line from The Rock to Oaklands (located about halfway between Sydney and Melbourne) with the Sunday morning news-papers on board.

In winter it was particularly exciting to go in with my father and stand on the Boree Creek platform, which was 491 feet (150 metres) above sea level and 375 miles (606 kilometres) south-west from Sydney Central, all accurately listed in the timetables of the era. Suddenly we would hear the rails start to hum and then the big single headlight beam would come around the corner and light up the station. The rust red railmotor would brake to a less than smooth halt and disgorge passengers, papers and small items of freight. Almost too quickly the whistle would blow and away it roared into the night, trying to adhere to its strict timetable: arrive Boree Creek, 6.52, depart 6.55 for Oaklands.

However, sometimes disaster did strike as was the case when someone forgot to load the newspapers onto the Riverina Daylight Express in Sydney or unload and reload them at The Rock junction. This was when I learnt to swear, listening to my dad and others let off steam on the platform! It was also when I became interested in learning about railways and how they worked.

So commenced a lifelong pursuit in studying rail, which I often weaved in with my various careers from farmer to transport officer in the army, from state politician to being a member of the Federal Parliament of Australia. My parliamentary life, if you can call it a life, extended over three decades with many portfolio and committee roles relating to trade and transport. It saw me travelling up the mighty Khyber Pass surrounded by guns on an ancient steam train. I've had the privilege of travelling in the driver's cabin on the TGV Atlantique out of Paris and the Shinkansen out of Tokyo. There were small and big openings of various railway lines such as the Pichi Richi back into Port Augusta, South Australia, and the chance to inspect freight operations around the world at places such as Dry Creek in South Australia and Xian in China.

Sometimes the stations and freight yards I visited wouldn't be there on return visits as cities such as Durban and Las Vegas moved them from downtown areas. At other times, I would annoy Australian ambassadors by asking to make early morning visits to main stations, a great way to assess the local standard of living and the economy. Having done this at sunrise at Pretoria, I went on to a meeting with then South African vice president Thabo Mbecki. To break the ice I asked when he had last been to Pretoria station. A big smile spread across his face. 'You should not ask this question,' he replied. 'It was 25 years ago and I was trying to blow the place up.' Some ice breaker. It took me a while to re-rail the talks.

This love of trains and railways, of stations and overseas travel has led me to think about rail at the start of the 21st century. The railways of the world readily divide into eleven realms, with many different gauges and cultures attaching. The railways in these realms often decided important moments of history and laid the groundwork for economic and political development.

Africa is at the top of the list with nearly as many gauges as colonial leaders. The controversial visionary Cecil Rhodes proposed the rail link from Cairo to Cape Town but it was never completed for various reasons, not the least of which was the break of gauge. The Stephenson standard gauge dominated in the north and Anglo Cape narrow gauge in the south. Still, Paul Theroux made it all the way through recently travelling by train and truck and everything else in between, with a new book to prove it.

Australia comes next as the world's only single nation continent. However, no less than 22 different railway gauges have been used since 1831, when the Australian Agricultural Company built Australia's very first railway at 'Newcastle-upon-Hunter'. Five main railway gauges dominated when two would have been sufficient. There have been some record-breaking feats since 1831 including the world's longest ever freight train which carried over 70 000 tonnes of iron ore between Mount Newman and Port Hedland in Western Australia's Pilbara. Australia led the world in developing double-decker suburban trains but is well behind the world in introducing high-speed trains. Since 1917 Australia has had one east–west transcontinental from Sydney to Perth but it took until 2004 for a south–north transcontinental from Adelaide to Darwin to be built. There remains the chance in the future of another transcontinental being built from Melbourne to Brisbane and then on to Mt Isa, Tennant Creek and Darwin.

China is a separate realm both because of its size and the huge potential for the growth of rail as its economy rapidly expands. China is currently building more new track than any other country in the world. Dominated by standard gauge internally, the break of gauge on its borders with both Russia and Vietnam has been useful at various times in the past for defence reasons, although it is less useful today. China has commenced building a new line across permafrost steppes to Lhasa, Tibet, but not without controversy or considerable engineering challenges.

Europe is the dynamic pace setter for high-speed trains, commuter and long-distance trains, with the world speed record of 526 kph being set by the French TGV Atlantique. Luckily, continental Europe's rail network is nearly all standard gauge, although Iberian broad dominates in Portugal and Spain, two colonial rivals of yesteryear. Narrow gauge tracks are sprinkled across mountain areas of France, Greece, Switzerland and on islands such as Sicily. Tiny trains with rack and pinion device below carriage to ensure grip can be seen tackling very steep grades with courage.

Great Britain is not only the birthplace of horse-hauled plateways and iron railways, but the place where in 1825 the first steam-hauled railway operations commenced between Stockton and Darlington and between Liverpool and Manchester in 1830. Engineered by father and son George and Robert Stephenson, both are regarded as the world's first true railways. The first death on the railway was also recorded in Great Britain when the president of the Board of Trade and MP for Liverpool, William Huskisson, was skittled during the opening ceremony of the Liverpool–Manchester railway by the steam locomotive Rocket as it passed the official train and the open carriage carrying the Duke of Wellington. Today Britain may well have one standard gauge but it has more than four different non-compatible electrification systems!

Even separating out the giants of China, India, East Russia and Japan, Greater Asia has the world's most diverse range of systems, stretching from the Grand Station of Istanbul to Surabaya in Indonesia. On my count there are at least eight gauges operating in Greater Asia, often in splendid isolation. Over the years some have been blown up by dynamite, others by less than dynamic operating policies. Lawrence of Arabia was kept busy during World War I blowing up the Damascus to Medina line. Given the fact it was a unique 3' 5⅜" perhaps he had the vision of one day seeing standard gauge sweep south from Damascus, as it is doing today, albeit rather slowly. The new Sky Train in Bangkok, Singapore's expanding metro and the fast airport service in Kuala Lumpur all attest to the importance of rail in this realm while the Eastern Oriental Express from Bangkok to Singapore says a lot about its splendour.

In India the just completed 'unigauge' project has converted the entire network to the Imperial broad gauge, apart from some smaller narrow gauge systems in the mountains such as the tiny, but superb, Darjeeling 'Toy Train'. The Imperial broad gauge was originally chosen by British viceroy, Lord Dalhousie, supposedly to stop the strong winds of the subcontinent blowing trains off the rails! Later it was found necessary to have a less costly version so Lord Mayo, who succeeded Viceroy Dalhousie, chose the narrow gauge system. India's railway system is so big it requires its own federal budget, which is generally presented the day before the national budget.

Japan showed how rail could leap into the future when it introduced the high-speed Shinkansen service on a standard gauge track. The Shinkansen often runs in parallel to the comprehensive narrow gauge track but travels at more than triple the speed, over 240 kilometres an hour, of the standard services. A Maglev magnetic track is now planned for the key Tokyo–Osaka route.

Russia went for 5' Czar broad gauge. This gauge was chosen by Czar Nicholas I around 1842 but the reasons are still debated to this day. Some say it was for defence purposes. The break of gauge between Russia and Poland certainly created blockages in resupply to the Russian Front during World War II. What we do know, however, is that the Czar was influenced by supervising engineer George Washington Whistler.

Whistler, a graduate of West Point Military Academy in the United States, moved to Russia in 1842 to help build the Czar's railways after he observed construction of 5' rail in the United States. Maybe Whistler and the Czar were simply trying to go one up on Queen Victoria and Great Britain by having a slightly wider gauge than Stephenson standard gauge. Today Russia struggles to modernise. Over 1.5 million people work on the railway, twice the number actually required I was once told in Moscow. Nevertheless, the world's longest major transcontinental link, the Trans-Siberian, was built by Russia and then double tracked in the early 20th century. It remains one of the world's great rail journeys.

The North American realm is, of course, dominated by the world's largest economy, that of the United States. Its extensive standard gauge freight networks work well but its passenger operation, Amtrak, is struggling. In the 19th century, the United States had no less than six separate operating gauges on the eastern seaboard alone. Fortunately this was rectified before the start of the 20th century, so that a standard gauge system operates across Canada, the United States and Mexico. Surprisingly, the world's first transcontinental line

was not across the United States but across Panama, some 80 kilo-
metres of rail completed in 1856 and still operating successfully today.
This transcontinental service effectively marks the border between
North and South America.

Finally realm number eleven, that of colourful and diverse South
America. The highest track in the world is in Peru, while two of the
world's grandest stations are the Retiro Station complex in Buenos
Aires and the Charles Eiffel designed Central Station in Santiago.
However, this realm is under stress with many important tracks
being closed as a result of economic crisis after economic crisis and
ongoing border tensions and flare-ups. The potential is there but
right now the urgently required capital for vital modernisation is
not.

Against this background it is time to ask if rail is still a relevant
mode of transport? Can it deliver in these turbulent economic times?
How exposed is it to terrorist activities and future wars? Can railway
systems cope with change and can operators depart deeply embedded comfort zones?

A retired colonel writing to the *London Times* many years ago had
no justifiable point when complaining about the removal of 'kippers'
from the British Rail breakfast menu. He never actually ordered
them but wanted the comfort of knowing that he could if he wanted
to on the few occasions he travelled to London by train rather than
car!

This is a great example of nostalgia that had to be challenged. In
Australia, the equivalent would be having a railmotor running daily
for an average of 2.5 passengers a month on the Gawler to Angaston
branch line in South Australia's Barossa Valley.

Let us now survey all the rail operators of today and their systems,
starting with the world's newest transcontinental from Adelaide to
Darwin. All aboard for a journey to the great railways of the world.

CHAPTER TWO

GAUGE BATTLES

There is nothing more pleasurable than a long-distance train journey. There is nothing more frustrating than that journey being broken with the screech of the locomotive and the cry, 'All change'. When visiting Australia in 1897, Mark Twain encountered one of the great stupidities of colonial Australia, the break of gauge on the Sydney to Melbourne Express. With bemused vigour, he reported:

> Now comes a singular thing: the oddest thing, the strangest thing, the most unaccountable marvel that Australia can show. At the frontier between NSW and Victoria our multitude of passengers were routed out of their snug beds by lantern light in the morning in the biting cold to change cars on a railroad that has no break in it from Sydney to Melbourne. Think of the paralysis of intellect that gave that idea birth; imagine the boulder it emerged from, on some petrified legislator's shoulders. It is a narrow gauge [sic] to the frontier and a broader gauge thence to Melbourne. One or two reasons are given for this curious state of things. One is that it represents the jealousy existing between the two colonies—the two most important colonies of Australasia. What the other is I have forgotten, it could be but another effort to explain the inexplicable.

It was at Albury on the New South Wales–Victoria border that the New South Wales standard gauge first met the Victorian Irish broad gauge with a very long platform in between. Furious with New South Wales for the original decision to go with standard gauge, Victoria demanded that the freight terminal be on its side of the border. A standard gauge track was therefore built alongside the Irish broad gauge across the Murray River and into the Victorian township of Wodonga. This still didn't satisfy the Victorians. At their insistence the Irish broad gauge track was pushed 100 yards past the Albury station into a silo siding where it came to a dead end.

I first encountered this matter of railway gauge as a young boy travelling to school from Albury to Melbourne in the early 1960s. These were exciting times for a school kid interested in trains. A decision had finally been made to build the standard gauge track all the way through to Melbourne. As each term passed, I watched it inch closer and closer towards Benalla, Mangalore Junction, Seymour and then Broadmeadow on the very outskirts of Melbourne.

My second encounter with break of railway gauge occurred when as a nineteen year old I joined two mates, Max Day and Graham Schirmer, on a trip around Australia in 1966. We had just finished planting the winter crops and headed off through Balranald to Marree in the middle of South Australia.

Most of the time this was harsh, drought-stricken country. The biggest development in the area was just to the south of Marree, the giant open-cut Leigh Creek coal mine. This project had justified upgrading to standard gauge the old Anglo Cape narrow gauge through the Pichi Richi Pass, Quorn, Government Gums and Marree so that the heavy loads of coal could be carried to the power station at the top of the Spencer Gulf near Port Augusta.

Max, Graham and I arrived in Marree on a late winter's afternoon and immediately found our way to the Marree Hotel to wait the arrival of the standard gauge Ghan from Port Augusta, due around 11.00 pm. Terminating at Marree, its passengers switched to the narrow gauge Old Ghan to Alice Springs, which was due to leave about an hour later.

We'd had a few rounds of drinks, and a meat pie or two when we heard the growling of the diesel locomotive. The penetrating searchlight mounted high on the locomotive could be easily seen a couple of kilometres distant in this flat, desolate country.

As the train rolled to a halt at the standard gauge terminus, I stumbled out of the bar to discover that my mates had already carefully loaded our car and all of our gear onto the flat top attached to the Alice Springs Ghan. I can still vividly recall a huge piece of partly carved roast beef being carefully transferred from the standard gauge dining car to narrow gauge buffet dining car and my sense of anticipation of substantial sustenance all the way through to Alice Springs.

For passengers originating in Adelaide, this was their second transfer: they had travelled Irish broad gauge from Adelaide to Port Pirie, then standard gauge from Port Pirie to Marree, and now they were on the last rickety narrow gauge stage. As if in compensation, the run from Marree to Oodnadatta across the Finke River and on into Alice Springs was in a magnificent set of old German carriages that were actually air-conditioned.

Despite the fact the carriages were built to standard gauge size and that they had to literally balance on narrow gauge replacement bogies, it was a comfortable journey. The train just kept rolling slowly along at around 25 miles (40 kilometres) per hour until the lights of Alice Springs loomed up out of the dark some 24 hours later.

I have to confess that by this stage Southwark, the main South Australian beer of the day, had wreaked havoc with me and I found myself on Alice Springs station with a well-embedded hangover. However, I still remember my real sense of excitement at having ridden the original narrow gauge Ghan. (This historic section of track was completely by-passed some fifteen years later.)

The next day, in the light of at least two pledges to give up the demon drink, I reflected on how crazy break of gauge was for

Australia and for many other countries around the world. It was a problem that was tackled head on by some countries in the late 19th century, but not in Australia.

Terrible mistakes were nearly made in 1902 and again in 2002—gauge mistakes that would have wrecked the Adelaide to Darwin railway project from the outset.

In the spring of 1902 the South Australian state parliament, meeting in Adelaide, debated at length the Transcontinental Railway Bill to connect Port Augusta and Adelaide through Marree, Alice Springs and Birdum to Port Elliot and Darwin. The bill offered an interesting incentive to those considering investing in the railway: they would be given ownership of the corridors of land adjoining the track for agricultural production. This incentive had been used in the United States in the early days of rail.

The bill's problem was a clause proposing the transcontinental be built in the somewhat restricting Anglo Cape narrow gauge. The bill eventually passed into law but a terrible drought between 1900 and 1904, then World War I, the Great Depression and World War II all delayed the project, and the Anglo Cape narrow gauge was never built through to Darwin.

Nearly one hundred years later, when track laying to Darwin commenced in earnest, a furious debate over gauge erupted on the lawn of Darwin's magnificent Mindil Beach Hotel. Don Williams, the former head of the Australian National Railways, contended that gauge was measured from the centre line of rail head to the centre line of rail head. Malcolm Kinnaird, who went on to head the Asia Pacific Transport syndicate for the Adelaide to Darwin transcontinental project, confirmed this was the normal engineering principle but that rail track gauge measurement was different.

Having studied rail in detail for decades, I immediately wagered that gauge was measured from inside rail face to inside rail face and that this has been so since George Stephenson chose his gauge width in the British Midlands in the early 19th century. I won the bet and mused on the disaster that might have been had the track been built

40 millimetres too narrow so that none of the existing rolling stock bogies would actually fit!

Why is this matter of gauge so important and how did it come about in the first place? Now, I allow that here is your chance to skip forward if you are not deeply interested in gauge, but remember wars have been won and lost on the matter.

The importance of gauge lies not in what it advanced but in the economic costs imposed by having so many different gauges. The differences owe much to misplaced patriotism, jealous engineers, ill-informed politicians and petty squabbling.

Gauge is, of course, a twofold dimension. The first, known as 'track gauge', is the width between the rails. The second, known as 'loading gauge', is the height and width of the locomotive or carriage (or more generally the rail rolling stock) above the surface of the rail, and the distance allowed between railway tracks side by side. Europe's above-track loading gauge, generally known as Berne loading gauge, is more generous than that of Great Britain.

Looking at the saga of gauge around the world, it is interesting to note that the United States started out in the 19th century with six different gauges along the eastern seaboard and across some of the southern states (4' 8½", 4' 10", 5', 5' 4", 5' 6" and 6'). New York alone had three different gauges. However, the two most extensively used gauges in the early days of rail in the United States were Czar broad gauge in the south (5' or 1524 mm) and standard gauge (4' 8½" or 1435 mm) in the north-east. Fierce competition broke out between the railway barons, people such as the redoubtable Commodore Cornelius Vanderbilt, as each tried to gain the ascendancy and capture more traffic on their railway with its particular gauge.

Britain is the birthplace of the modern rail-mounted steam locomotive. (In 1804 Richard Trevithick ran the world's first steam locomotive from the iron works at Penydarren to the Merthyr-Cardiff Canal.) It is also where standard gauge, Stephenson standard, emerged between 1825 and 1840. As Michael Robbins details in *The*

Railway Age, and as backed up by everything from the *Dumpy Book of Rail* to direct inspection, the first Stephenson standard gauge was not exactly 4' 8½".

Stephenson's Stockton and Darlington railway was designed and built, according to Michael Robbins, 'patterned on the Killingworth Wagonway at four feet eight inches or 1418 millimetres'. The Liverpool–Manchester Railway Board papers for this first major public railway, built in 1825, declared a gauge of 4' 8" as did the 1828 amending legislation in Westminster. To help the rail wheels negotiate the curves, a short time later Stephenson standard gauge drifted out by just half an inch to become the usual 4' 8½". In modern times, however, there has been a slight narrowing of standard gauge as engineers have taken advantage of the greater precision available, so that on some tracks it has been brought in by 3 mm (or ¼") to 1432 mm.

It has been said over and over again that Stephenson used the old Roman chariot wheel tracks, reflected in local plate ways and wagon ways, to determine his gauge width. MG Lay supports this theory in his book *On the Way of the World*, arguing that the 'Roman Ruts' were always between 1150 and 1450 millimetres across as this distance suited the axles of the chariots. A similar standard width (1500 mm) was adopted by the Chinese Emperor Shi in 221 BC. Clearly, this width was very practical. More significantly, the moulds and lathes used by blacksmiths and in foundries in Stephenson's time were geared to carriage wheels and wagon wheels with 4' 8" axles.

Whatever the reason, Stephenson's standard gauge was found to work well and was soon used far and wide. It quickly took hold in the north and in the midlands of Great Britain and was widely adopted in many countries around the world.

There is an often repeated story that standard gauge is exactly the arse width of two horses pulling a chariot side by side. An Internet twist suggests that as the booster rockets used in the United States' space program had to be transported by rail to Florida, the shape of 21st century space equipment owes something to the Roman Empire in the first century AD!

Let me advance a new theory on why Stephenson standard started at 4' 8". It is both simple and compelling, is not dissimilar to the Killingworth Wagonway theory and is based on the easiest and most accurate way to measure a rail, that is from outside edge to outside edge using an early version of a track caliper. It is more than likely that Stephenson's standard measurement from outside edge to outside edge was a neat 5', being completely compatible with local moulds and lathes. Given the 2" (51 mm) width of rail head at that time, the actual gauge from inside of rail to inside of rail would have been 4' 8".

Some would say this is nonsense and heresy, but I believe it is a theory not able to be entirely rejected. Robert Lee, who has written several books on rail, including a classic on John Whitton entitled *Colonial Engineer*, also supports this idea.

Those who make history, and clearly George Stephenson is very much in that category, rarely have time to take a step back and consider every aspect of their work as it develops. Stephenson, ever the practical engineer, made one adjustment of half an inch, and then with son Robert conquered much of the world, leaving Isambard Kingdom Brunel's ultra broad 7' ¼" (2140 mm) gauge behind.

Robert laid out the route of one of the very early passenger railways, the Canterbury and Whitstable, sometimes called the Crab and Winkle, which opened on 3 May 1830. His Liverpool and Manchester railway opened a few months later on 15 September. The Crab and Winkle combined gravity downhill sections with steam-powered cable haul uphill, while carriages on the Liverpool and Manchester were locomotive hauled for its full length. History therefore records, quite correctly, that the first locomotive-hauled proper passenger train ran on the longer Liverpool and Manchester.

In the mid 19th century the British parliament commissioned a major study to settle the issue as to whether Stephenson standard was better or worse than Isambard Kingdom Brunel's ultra broad gauge. Britain's rail network was expanding rapidly, especially in the period leading up to the Great London Exhibition of 1851, and break of gauge problems were emerging in the southern counties. At Bristol Temple Meads terminating trains from London's Paddington station used Brunel ultra broad gauge as did through trains to Dawlish and Penzance. Terminating trains from the Midlands, on the other hand, were on Stephenson standard gauge track. Different platforms were required for each operation.

On technical grounds, the study found in favour of Brunel's ultra broad gauge as it offered more stability without too much extra cost. But before Brunel could celebrate, a final ruling was made in favour of Stephenson standard. By now, Stephenson standard dominated track length in Great Britain and too much had already been laid to consider removing it. The Great Western Railway had to shift all its rails in from Brunel ultra broad to Stephenson standard. This was completed in 1892. The whole of Paddington station and its marshalling yards were changed over in one weekend. Sadly not one set of dual gauge platform tracks were kept for posterity. Today, short display sections can be found at Didcot Great Western Railway Museum and York National Railway Museum.

Robert Stephenson took up where his father left off and pushed standard gauge around the world. He travelled everywhere from Colombia to Egypt and many places in between, and railway after railway adopted Stephenson standard gauge. Apart from Portugal and Spain, Continental Europe soon followed Great Britain. Then came Argentina and Peru and later China.

In the United States, the push west to California was continuing. The influence of Mexican mission settlements extended up as far as San Francisco and Sonoma, and the Russian influence extended down from Alaska. As the concepts of the east–west transcontinental emerged in the aftermath of the Civil War, and with the security concerns in mind, it became obvious that the railways should operate on one gauge.

In 1861 the United States Congress approved the first east–west transcontinental. This standard gauge railway linked up at Promontory, Utah in 1869. Most of the existing track was converted to standard gauge by 1890, although the loading gauge above track was much larger than that in Britain.

All the railway realms of the world made the mistake of developing different gauges. While this was justified in mountainous regions where the narrow gauge allowed for sharper curves, only the United States and Great Britain moved quickly to correct the problem. (Having said this, however, a multitude of narrow and very narrow gauges emerged when one, such as Suez Walhalla Whitfield narrow [2' 6" or 762 mm] would have sufficed.) India gradually fixed the problem in the 20th century; Australia is still in the process of doing so.

The petty jealousies in 19th century Australia appeared to be worse than anywhere else when it came to gauge. For its first railway line, between Sydney and Parramatta, New South Wales initially chose standard gauge. This decision was supported by Victoria in the knowledge that one day both systems would link. However, in 1850 an Irish engineer and surveyor, Francis Shields, arrived in New South Wales. He made the decision to adopt Irish broad gauge (5' 3" or 1600 mm). This was a less than smart move, given the seething jealousy between Sydney and Melbourne, although in a generous decision Victoria also switched its planning to Irish broad. It all came unstuck, however, when the Irish engineer resigned and New South Wales appointed a Scottish engineer, James Wallace, who chose to go back to standard gauge.

Now this was too much for the colony of Victoria. Objecting to the lack of consultation, it decided to continue with the Irish broad gauge. So the two most populous colonies of Australia went their own ways, although Victoria at least decided to put its lengthy network of Melbourne tram tracks down at standard gauge!

As it turned out, the New South Wales track met the wider Victorian track at just three locations—Albury, Oaklands and Tocumwal, all in southern New South Wales. Nevertheless, having Australia's two largest cities without a seamless railway connection was a big disadvantage, as Mark Twain discovered.

South Australia elected to adopt two gauges, selecting the Irish broad in 1851 and Anglo Cape (3' 6" or 1067 mm) for the more sparsely populated areas in the 1860s. This decision was no doubt influenced by Isambard Kingdom Brunel, who South Australia appointed as English agent and consulting engineer. He was known to favour anything other than Stephenson standard. This led to break of gauge problems north of Adelaide, most notably at Terowie on the Adelaide to Broken Hill railway line.

The editor of the Port Augusta *Dispatch* wrote scathingly about smaller gauges, stating in one editorial 'we accept the narrow gauge in the same spirit as the beggar receives the half loaf'! By 1917 Port Augusta had both narrow and standard, although never Irish broad. This was to be the dubious privilege reserved for nearby Gladstone, which had all three for a few years.

Against formidable odds, Australia's east–west transcontinental was completed in 1917 in the middle of the worst phase of World War I. It was built in standard gauge. This was a remarkable federal decision, because at this time neither South Australia nor Western Australia had standard gauge railways. (Anglo Cape narrow gauge was used for the early railways in Western Australia, including Perth to Fremantle.) Credit for this decision must go to Henry Deane, New South Wales' railways engineer and later federal chief engineer. Deane had vast railway construction experience in the United Kingdom, where he was born, and in eastern Europe and the Philippines and was very much a believer in standard gauge.

Although Tasmania started with Irish broad gauge, it eventually decided to go narrow, while Queensland elected to go with Anglo Cape narrow gauge from the outset. In fact, Queensland built the first narrow gauge main line in the world from Ipswich west of Brisbane over the Great Dividing Range to Toowoomba.

Engineer Abraham Fitzgibbon convinced the Queensland government that narrow gauge would allow the big and sparsely populated colony to benefit from a lower cost railway. Fitzgibbon was also influenced by the Great Dividing Range, which had to be crossed by the very first section of railway built in Queensland. This involved no less than 47 bridges and nine tunnels between Helidon and Harlaxton just before Toowoomba.

Only Norway had adopted Anglo Cape narrow gauge at the time it was taken up by Queensland. What Queensland proved was that narrow or medium gauge could be utilised for long-distance main line train operation. To this day Queensland feels short changed about its lack of recognition, given that the colony was a railway pioneer setting the way for Indonesia, Japan and South Africa. Perhaps the Anglo Cape narrow gauge should have been called Fitzgibbon narrow or simply Queensland narrow. Much later, between the two world wars, a standard gauge line was built from New South Wales to south Brisbane. The standard gauge was finally pushed across the Brisbane River into Roma Street station, Brisbane's main station, well after World War II.

The Northern Territory's one railway line ran from Darwin down the track to Birdum. It too was Anglo Cape narrow gauge. The line was closed not long after Cyclone Tracy devastated Darwin on Christmas Day 1974.

Since 1831, when the Australian Agricultural Company built the first railway in Australia in Newcastle, no less than 22 different gauges have operated (and some continue to operate) on lines of 1.6 kilometres or longer, ranging from the Irish broad to the extremely narrow gauge of 1' 3" (381 mm) at Bush Mill in Tasmania. Sometimes parliaments involved themselves in lengthy debates to formulate gauge. This was the case in Victoria when the state parliament adopted the Suez Walhalla Whitfield narrow gauge for the famous Puffing Billy line east of Melbourne.

The unique (German) Monash narrow gauge (2' 11³/₈" or 900 mm) 12.75 kilometre long line was designed by General Sir John Monash to open up Victoria's huge Latrobe Valley brown coal deposits. Australia's most successful general on the Western Front during World War I, Monash learnt European coal processing techniques, particularly brown coal production, in Germany and his gauge reflected

German mining practice. Unfortunately, the railway was closed at the end of the 20th century due to a coal pit realignment.

Another railway 'world first' exists between Northam and Perth in Western Australia along the Avon Valley. In the quest for standardisation, the existing Anglo Cape narrow gauge was moved to a new alignment and revamped to a double track while a standard gauge line was laid as a third rail. The passing loops, which are also dual gauge and were installed between the tracks, have a very complex set of entry points. This line remains hopelessly over-engineered for the amount of traffic it gets. It is, however, a train spotter's delight when the Hotham Valley steam train passes the long Indian Pacific passenger train, while a bulk grain train waits patiently in the loop.

Despite all the efforts taken to standardise gauge in Australia, in 2002 Irish broad gauge was still being built in Victoria. The Great Port Echuca railway is the world's newest Irish broad gauge branch line, running from Echuca's main station down to the Murray River wharf. Opened in the spring of 2002 with a steam engine hauling a delightful two-carriage train, the scene became slightly bizarre when we realised a diesel locomotive was up the back pushing the train for safety.

Unfortunately, the very dedicated Irish ambassador to Australia was not at the opening. Perhaps it was because I had suggested he bring a dozen bottles of Irish whisky with him and that he swim the Murray!

All in all, there are currently twelve major gauges and six minor (narrow) gauges used on operating railways in the world today. From largest, or widest, to smallest they are: Imperial broad (5' 6" or 1676 mm), Iberian broad (5' 5^2/$_3$" or 1668 mm), Irish broad (5' 3" or 1600 mm), Czar broad (5' or 1524 mm), Stephenson standard (4' 8^1/$_2$" or 1435 mm), Anglo Cape narrow (3' 6" or 1067 mm), Mid-East narrow (3' 5^3/$_8$" or 1050 mm), metre (3' 3^3/$_8$" or 1000 mm), Italian narrow (3' 1^1/$_2$" or 950 mm), Americas narrow (3' or 915 mm), Suez

Walhalla Whitfield narrow (2' 6" or 762 mm) and Cane narrow (2' or 610 mm).

In the very narrow category, I will settle on: Decauville or Eastern Europe metric mini narrow (1' 11⅝" or 600 mm), beach narrow Britain or Tasmania (1' 3" or 381 mm), Bosnian narrow (2' 5⅞" or 760 mm), Swedish narrow (2' 11" or 891 mm), Switzerland narrow (2' 7½" or 800 mm), and Patagonian (Argentina Brazil Euro) narrow (2' 5½" or 750 mm). Any narrower than these and you would be enjoying one of the many wonderful garden tourist railways around the world. Operated by thousands of committed volunteers, whose enthusiasm is often difficult for outsiders to understand, these railways are built with a love of railway history and railway culture.

If we were able to start afresh to build railways around the world today, two gauges would suffice instead of 22. These would be Irish broad gauge for main lines and the narrow metre gauge, included for steep mountain routes, but I do accept that the great grandfather of all railways, George Stephenson, might have a totally different view!

PART ONE

AUSTRALIAN FOUNDATIONS

CHAPTER THREE

GREEN LIGHT TO DARWIN

For all that successful railway projects will have many thousands of patrons, the truth is that more often than not only a handful of people will be responsible for that success, and they will have been helped along with a bit of luck. This is the case with Australia's two trans-continental railways, which run east–west from Sydney to Perth and now south–north from Adelaide to Darwin.

A tangle of transcontinental railway proposals for Australia emerged in the 19th century. One of the earliest was to build a single great diagonal transcontinental line running from Sydney to Collier Bay north of Broome at the very top end of Western Australia. This was a strange proposal that would have seen existing tracks used from Sydney across the Blue Mountains to Dubbo and Bourke, then across far south-west Queensland. As if an omen, it was proposed that the line would then cross over the mighty Cooper Creek near the Burke and Wills Dig Tree, the scene of one of the most poignant tragedies in Australian exploration history. One way or another this giant diag-onal transcontinental was never built. Had this imaginative proposal succeeded, Australia's most isolated roadhouse, the famous Rabbit Flat Roadhouse along the Tanami Track and operated for years by the Farrand family, may well have been a wayside stop and siding and refreshment rooms!

There are many remnants of Australia's railway ambitions scattered around the country, including the road bridge near Yelta Siding across the Murray River, downstream of Mildura. Now known as the Abbotsford Bridge, it was all set to carry Victoria's Irish broad gauge line onwards from Mildura to Broken Hill, close to Mount Isa, and thence to Darwin but it was not to be. There was no way the New South Wales government of the day was going to allow the Victorian government to run its track across the state to Queensland. So the rail came all the way up from Melbourne and Geelong but stopped less than 5 kilometres short of the large and well-designed rail-road bridge at the state border, as if in fright at entering New South Wales.

Another proposal out of Victoria was to head due north from Echuca on the Murray River to Cobar and Bourke then Mount Isa and on to Darwin. Halted by the economic slow down of the 1890s, two Irish broad gauge tracks were built north of Echuca into New South Wales, one to Deniliquin and one to Balranald on the Murrumbidgee River.

The Balranald line gained some notoriety many years later when, on Christmas Eve 1962, a fettler loading up supplies, including the Christmas beer order, accidentally put the rail trolley in gear. The driverless trolley took off down the track, hurtling past the Caldwell general store on collision course with the Balranald railmotor. The quick-thinking storekeeper, John Vagg, chased the runaway trolley in his car and threw together a quickly erected barrier of disused sleepers, derailing the trolley and smashing all the beer on board. A few minutes later the Balranald railmotor came into view, the crew and passengers none the wiser of the near miss. One very embarrassed fettler was left to explain why there would be no beer for Christmas, a disaster that has become part of local folklore.

Many of the early proposals for a transcontinental railway were simply on wish lists. However, during the 1890s as the six Australian colonies worked towards Federation, the drive for a transcontinental railway began in earnest. Western Australia, with its deep-seated dislike of the so-called 'great wise men from the east', was suspicious of the motives of the other Australian colonies, while Queensland was opposed outright, believing a transcontinental railway would divert its scarce resources and be of little benefit.

The breakthrough was engineered by Western Australian premier and treasurer, Sir John Forrest, who bargained an east–west transcontinental railway for his state's support of Federation. The politically influential goldminers around Kalgoorlie, with whom Sir John was in close contact, looked to a direct railway link between the west and the goldfields of Ballarat and Bendigo in the east in preference to a hazardous journey on coastal steamers and sailing ships of the era. Unfortunately the east–west railway was not written into the Constitution of Australia.

In 1901 Sir John was elected to the new federal parliament then sitting in Melbourne. At every opportunity, both in government and in opposition, he pushed the cause. (The best are always destined to spend periods in opposition. Churchill, Menzies, Hawke and Howard are all better for having spent a period there.)

Fourteen days after the federal parliament assembled for the first time on 9 May 1901, the new Member for Swan was on his feet claiming that Western Australians would never be happy 'unless we give them means of communication by a railway'. He threatened to 'undo' this Federation if a railway was not forthcoming. These remarks created a useful uproar and Forrest was accused of treason.

However, the transcontinental was not to be a burning priority for members from the eastern states and, a little like the east–west transcontinental in the United States, there were to be many false starts, some scandals and much political meddling. The location of rich goldfields had a big bearing on the ultimate route of the railways in both continents. The huge gold fields around Kalgoorlie and, to a lesser extent, around Tarcoola in central South Australia resulted in the east–west transcontinental taking a northerly route, instead of hugging the coastline of the Great Australian Bight. Likewise, and despite fierce lobbying, gold strikes in California and Nevada saw the first transcontinental line in the United States go through the middle of the country rather than take an extreme northern or southern route.

In 1904 Sir John Forrest introduced the Transcontinental Survey Bill into the House of Representatives where it was passed only to be rejected by the Senate. In what became a game of political poker between the federal government and South Australia and Western Australia, the bill was rejected again in 1906 with a tied vote of 13 all. This sinister set of numbers only increased the resolve of the proponents.

On 28 August 1907 the bill finally passed both Houses, and as many have pointed out, including David Burke in his book *Road Through the Wilderness: The story of the transcontinental, the first great work of Australia's Federation*, by now it involved more than the £20 000 requested for a survey in the original bill. The project had been given a green light by the federal parliament.

Meanwhile there were even bigger changes in the air as South Australia prepared to surrender the area now known as the Northern Territory to the Commonwealth of Australia. South Australian premier Tom Price locked a north–south railway from Darwin to South Australia into the state surrender and federal acceptance legislation.

However, no timetable was laid out for either project, and the solemn undertakings of the Commonwealth drifted along. Not even two world wars brought about action on the Darwin front, but concerns over defence and security did prompt action on the east–west railway. In 1911 Australia had the dubious pleasure of a visit from Herbert Horatio Kitchener, the Boer War general and chief of the Imperial General Staff who initiated the curious and disputed court martial of three Australians, including Breaker Morant, for killing Boer prisoners and civilians. Breaker Morant and Peter Handcock were shot at dawn not far from Pretoria Railway Station. The third Australian, George Witton, had his sentence commuted to life. Years later he was released from incarceration in the United Kingdom at the behest of thousands of petitioners, including

Australia's first native-born governor-general Sir Isaac Isaacs and Sir Winston Churchill.

Lord Kitchener urged Australia to build an east–west railway, otherwise it would be 'helpless against any aggressor who is able to mount an attack'. The current rail network layout, he said, was more helpful to the invading enemy than the defenders. Today a side chapel in a distant corner of St Paul's Cathedral London is dedicated to Kitchener, who was lost at sea in the darkest days of World War I while on a secret mission to Russia.

As if in salute, a small railway siding 265 kilometres east of Kalgoorlie was named after Lord Kitchener. It may, however, eventually face a name change, the result of efforts launched after a 2001 ceremonial 'Tracks to Federation' Indian Pacific journey in 2001.

I must confess to being the prime instigator. I had just finished reading a manuscript by Nick Bleszynski on the saga of Breaker Morant and was somewhat angry about Kitchener's role. As we passed that siding on the Nullarbor and in the comfort of the Indian Pacific lounge car, it was not hard to have one more toast to the cause of renaming the Kitchener Siding the Morant Siding.

In one of those twists of fate, on that same journey we alighted at Ooldea Siding several sidings to the east of the Morant/Kitchener Siding for a terrific midnight ceremony in salute of Australia's Federation centenary. There stood a monument to the famous Daisy Bates, who was for a time married to the Breaker.

In the same year following Kitchener's visit the Kalgoorlie to Port Augusta Bill (1911) was introduced to the federal parliament by King O'Malley. This time with the drumbeat of defence and security and the need to hold the Federation together the bill was passed into legislation. The east–west link was at last given full steam ahead with construction commencing in 1912. Notwithstanding World War I, Australia's first transcontinental railway was completed in 1917.

It was a huge stroke of luck, combined with some strategic planning, that the northerly option across the Nullarbor was adopted, as this helped lay the foundation for the Alice Springs standard gauge link at Tarcoola and the Adelaide to Darwin transcontinental railway many years later.

So, by 1917, the two big building blocks for the Adelaide to Darwin transcontinental had been put in place: a common gauge, namely standard gauge, and one-quarter of the track to Tarcoola. Another quarter of the track was built in the 1970s when the Tarcoola line was extended to Alice Springs.

The Tarcoola to Alice Springs project was started by the Whitlam government. Gough Whitlam travelled to Tarcoola to turn the first sod with his transport minister Charlie Jones in a special train hauled by two locomotives, each of which was named after the prime minister and the minister. (It was a Commonwealth Railways practice to name diesel locomotives after prime ministers and federal transport ministers.) Throughout his political career Gough Whitlam was very strongly committed to a federal role in the development of rail.

The railway to Alice Springs was completed under the Fraser–Anthony government when Ralph Hunt was federal transport minister. Hunt was part of a famous, some would say infamous, troika of 20th century National Party transport ministers that included Peter Nixon and Ian Sinclair. All three made a subtle contribution to the development of Australia's transcontinental railways by allowing vital survey work to keep going right through to Darwin and by turning a blind eye to Keith Smith, the long-serving and very successful head of the Commonwealth Railways from 1960 to 1981. Smith managed a huge upgrading of the east–west transcontinental, virtually under the nose of the parsimonious federal Treasury, by doing it in stages over several years. Had Smith applied for a one-off allocation to upgrade to concrete sleepers, Treasury and cabinet would have no doubt refused funding.

The Tarcoola to Alice Springs link had a right royal opening just south of Alice Springs in 1980, when Princess Alexandra did the honours. This left a gap of 'just' 1420 kilometres to Darwin and one helluva lot of political wrangling to be overcome. The history of this wrangling spread well over a century.

Back in 1872, when the Overland Telegraph from Darwin through to Adelaide was completed, communication between Australia and London and Europe was reduced from up to four months by ship to just four hours by telegraph. With this, a north–south corridor started to emerge in Australia.

Then in 1876, the colony of South Australia, which stretched from Mount Gambier in the far south to Melville Island north of Darwin, legislated for an Imperial narrow gauge railway to run from Port Augusta at the top of the Spencer Gulf to Government Gums (now called Farina), just south of Marree. The railway was to travel from the coastal plains and salt pans of the Gulf via the beautiful Pichi Richi Pass continuing north past Quorn.

When South Australian governor Sir William Jervois turned the first sod at Port Augusta in fiercely hot conditions in early 1878, he thought way into the future by noting that the railway was not just going to Port Darwin but to 'Java, India, Siam and China'. 'Rail to Asia' was well and truly launched over a century before it became a reality.

At the Top End, South Australian legislation in 1883 provided for the start of the Northern Australia Railway, a narrow gauge track from Palmerston (Darwin) down to the Adelaide and Katherine rivers ultimately reaching a dead halt at Birdum where it could have joined the track from Farina in the south.

The northern railway had some busy periods, particularly at its inception and during World War II. But it was not until the 1960s when Sir Frank Duval, who had served in the Occupying Forces in Japan, started to export iron ore by rail from Frances Creek Mine to Darwin and thence to Japan that it experienced a real mini boom. One of the workers upgrading the track at the time was a newly arrived migrant from Scotland, Robert Goldie. He was so 'hot and bothered' by the fierce humidity and the very high temperatures that he only lasted a week. 'You could drink two water bags a day but you still did not have to go,' he recalled many years later from the cool safety of Sydney's Bronte Beach.

Shortly after Cyclone Tracy devastated Darwin on Christmas Day 1974, both the Frances Creek Mine branch line and the Northern Australia Railway were closed. The Frances Creek Mine line was knocked off by larger and more efficient mines in the Pilbara of Western Australia using heavier trains on standard gauge. By way of compensation for the closure of the northern railway, the Fraser–Anthony Coalition government decided to push on with standardisation on the new flood-free alignment from Tarcoola to Alice Springs.

In 1902, the South Australian government made one last attempt to complete the north–south transcontinental link when it formally passed the Transcontinental Railway Bill in the spring of 1902. The bill was never implemented, which was a good thing as the narrow gauge track it provided for would have been a disaster for future rail operations, but particularly for container freight.

Things were somewhat dormant on the north–south front for several decades but eventually the narrow gauge was extended to Alice Springs from the south in 1929. The Great Depression and drought then hit hard.

In 1937 the Commonwealth extended the standard gauge from Port Augusta to Port Pirie. Suddenly travelling time on the section from Port Augusta to Adelaide was reduced from 12 hours to 5½ hours. (Today, depending on rail traffic, travel time is faster again on the standard gauge single track, helped by a short section of double track between Crystal Brook and Port Pirie.)

The big gap in the north–south transcontinental link (between Darwin and Alice Springs) that remained became a logistical nightmare during World War II. However, in one memorable moment the platform at Terowie gained a place in Australian history when General Douglas MacArthur uttered the line, 'I will return' as he changed from the narrow to broad gauge track. These words were, of course, directed at driving the Japanese back and returning to the Philippines, not to the tiny town of Terowie.

By the time the general reached Spencer Street Station in

Melbourne, thousands of frightened Australians were on hand to welcome him in the darkest days of World War II. Arguably this was the southernmost point of his journey, where the retreat ended and the general turned north to regroup and face the enemy.

On this famous journey south from Darwin to Melbourne in March 1942 MacArthur, who travelled with his family, was offered the best food, the best drinks and, of course, the Commissioner's best carriages. For Stuart Holland and Ollie McHugh, the drivers of the special train from Alice Springs, there were also some benefits, including the delight of the superior rations supplied by the Americans. (Some things never change, as I remember from the war in Vietnam.) 'That Yankee tinned stuff was out of this world,' Stuart Holland told the *Australian* in March 2002. For Prime Minister John Curtin, who received MacArthur in Canberra, the general's many train changes would have been a sharp reminder of the great inefficiencies created by the breaks of gauge.

After the war, public works priorities turned to other projects such as the construction of the massive Snowy Mountains Hydroelectric Scheme. However, there was renewed talk of a rail project from Townsville to Darwin and the idea of a standard gauge link from South Australia through to Alice Springs hadn't disappeared.

During the 1950s and 1960s, the Northern Territory began to see its tourism industry take off, especially after sealed roads were completed to Ayers Rock (now known by its traditional name Uluru) and the Olgas. Mining and pastoral industries also expanded rapidly. It became obvious to many that a railway from Adelaide to Darwin could only open up the Territory even more. One very early proponent of a transcontinental railway was Reverend John Flynn, Flynn of the Inland.

In June 1954 Prime Minister Robert Menzies visited Alice Springs to lay the foundation stone for the John Flynn Memorial Church. Next door, the ever practical Reverend John Flynn had built Adelaide House with its natural flow-through air circulation system.

Back in 1912 he had completed a trail-blazing report into the problems and economic prospects of inland Australia.

Reverend John Flynn was appointed the first superintendent of the Inland Mission and was founder of the Royal Flying Doctor Service, providing medical services to the people of the outback. Both were important in the early development of the Territory. What was missing was a railway. 'If Australians are to have any part in the development of the Territory', he said, 'I am certain that railway communication with the rest of the Commonwealth must be given at an early date'. Later he simply stated, 'We want railways'.

In 1923, as part of his campaign, he drew up a couple of maps comparing the development of railways in Australia with railways in the United States. Under the map of Australia he listed 26 345 miles of railway and observed this was 'a little more than enough to stretch around the Earth'. Under the map of the United States, he bluntly noted: 'End on USA railways would circle the world fifteen times, 375 000 miles and all in one gauge!' The railway made it into Alice Springs in 1929.[1]

John Flynn was also a remote area photographer. His magnificent but now fragile collection records so much of the development of the Australian outback. One photo taken in 1926, and now held safely by the National Library of Australia, is of the early mixed train that operated before the Ghan started running.

While progress was being made on many practical fronts and there was some popular support, the political will to get on with building the south–north transcontinental was still not there. In fact, in 1961 the South Australian government took the Commonwealth to the High Court of Australia in an attempt to gain compliance with the by then 50-year-old Commonwealth legislation to build the transcontinental. Unfortunately, but correctly, the High Court ruled

---

1. This was the same year the first eight pedal radio transmitters, developed by radio technician Alf Traeger and John Flynn, were distributed. Alf Traeger teamed up with John Flynn to find an alternative to the unreliable battery-operated radios used for all communication in the outback. The pedal-operated radio changed life in Australia's remotest regions forever.

there had never been any stipulation of a starting date or timetable for completion.

In the 1970s the Northern Territory was granted a form of self-government, with its own chief minister, ministers and assembly. It in turn began to lobby afresh for the railway only to be faced in 1977 with a report from the federal Bureau of Transport Economics recommending upgrading the highway from Alice Springs to Darwin instead of a rail link. In response, the ruling Country–Liberal Party appointed Barry Coulter as minister of railways to spearhead the project.

In 1983 Prime Minister Malcolm Fraser announced the Commonwealth would build the Alice Springs to Darwin railway as an extension to the existing standard gauge track from Tarcoola to Alice Springs, which had been operating since 1980. Malcolm Fraser was so eager to get things moving that he rang the minister, Ralph Hunt, who was taking a compulsory leave break on the Gold Coast. We must have this railway, Malcolm Fraser said down the phone. A Cabinet submission was very quickly produced.

However, this was an election year and in March the Fraser government was thrown out of office. Bob Hawke was swept in as prime minister with the sometimes deeply negative Paul Keating as federal treasurer. Soon after, the project was stopped about two kilometres to the north-west of the existing Alice Springs railway station in a lonely part of the Todd River Basin now used for trail bike riding. The tracks just vanished into a two-metre high wall of dirt and remained this way for 20 years.

As with every political backflip, various reports were commissioned, dare I say, to cover tracks! First there was the David Hill report of 1984 and then the Neville Wran report in 1994. Both found there would be a negative rate of return, but Wran at least was optimistic about the prospects of rail. Eventually, in 1999, a Booz-Allen and Hamilton report found a positive rate of return could be achieved, thus bolstering the political will to get on with the completion of the north–south link.

It was at this time that governments began looking at partnerships with private enterprise to build big projects. How was the federal Coalition government, which had swept into office in March 1996 under John Howard's leadership, going to fund this project in the difficult budgetary times?

A tough election year loomed in 1998 and the centenary of Federation year was quickly approaching in 2001. At the last cabinet meeting of 1997 John Howard, in a brilliant move, announced the creation of the Federation Fund, a bank of $1 billion for projects that would help commemorate the formation of the Commonwealth of Australia.

This allowed the federal government to offer an initial $100 million to push the railway through from Alice Springs to Darwin. I took the call from the Prime Minister confirming the offer on a mobile at the Townsville Rugby League Stadium, home of the Cowboys! I was always a little wary when getting unexpected phone calls from the prime minister, but this one was an absolute joy. He and the Treasurer had given the project the big tick. The timing was linked, in part, to the election campaign then taking place in South Australia.

It was ironic that I was in Townsville when this call came through, as Townsville was one of the starting points for a very early proposal to build a railway to Darwin. Much later, in the 1970s, Queensland Premier Sir Joh Bjelke-Petersen, together with mining magnate Lang Hancock, proposed an east–west transcontinental across northern Australia. It was envisaged Queensland coal would go west and Western Australian iron ore would go east. It was also not to be, due mainly to insufficient financial support.

At last real political progress was being made and negotiations began in earnest between the federal government and the South Australian and Northern Territory governments. There was light not so much at the end of the tunnel, but up the track and it was not just a heat mirage.

In June 1999 it was announced that Asia Pacific Transport had won the tender to build and operate Australia's first north–south railway under the auspices of the AustralAsia Railway Corporation, which had been set up by the South Australian and Northern Territory governments in 1997. Chaired by a shrewd engineer and sailor, Malcolm Kinnaird, the Adelaide-based Asia Pacific Transport board included Nick Bowen, the new, young and dynamic CEO of MacMahon Holdings.[2]

After some long and complex negotiations, the prime minister, John Howard, South Australian Premier John Olsen and Northern Territory Chief Minister Denis Burke signed the contract to begin work on 18 October 2000. On 20 April 2001, the federal and Northern Territory governments provided additional funding and committed a total of $330 million. The South Australian government also provided $150 million in financial support.

Asia Pacific Transport sensibly divided the giant task into two, setting up ADrail as the design and construction organisation and FreightLink as the operator. Also involved at commencement of the project were Kellog Brown and Root, Australian Railroad Group, John Holland Group, Barclay Mowlem, MacMahon Holdings and SANT Logistic Group. Colonial Investment Services, National Asset Management of the National Australian Bank and the Northern Territory government were also direct equity investors.

In a significant gesture indicating the strong support of indigenous communities, both the Central and Northern Aboriginal Investment Corporations also became involved. This commitment was vital and helped in many ways, including in clearing the way for the track corridor through areas subject to complex native title claims.

At the coalface were hands-on engineers and project leaders with a wide range of experience in major infrastructure projects such as the Mascot railway project to Sydney Airport. As CEOs, Franco Moretti in Adelaide and Al Volpe in Darwin both played a critical role

---

2. In addition to godfathers Kinnaird and Bowen, the original board and guiding fathers of the project's initial phase were Geoff Coffey, Andrew Fletcher, Peter Gunn, Brett Lazarides, Doug Ridley, Ron Thomas and Philip Williams.

in negotiating all aspects of the project. Design engineer Charles Duncan and construction manager Kevyn Brown all led large and dedicated teams. If Moretti was dubbed the Brunel of the project, Volpe, Duncan and Brown might be dubbed the Stephensons of the project. Project superintendent Bob Cush dealt with some huge logistical problems, including pre-positioning two million concrete sleepers to a very tight schedule.

Duncan Beggs led a small team which had to deal with a wide range of community relations issues including corridor and level crossing issues and the vigorous lobbying of a railway heritage group at historic Adelaide River. This group succeeded in having the main line lowered slightly and shifted two metres to the east to maintain the vistas and improve operations, a wonderful example of David winning over Goliath. Franco Moretti played a not insignificant role in having the line moved after he received an earful from the locals during a meal stop at Adelaide River. Unfortunately, not everyone was happy, reflecting the relentless but not always realistic passions of rail heritage enthusiasts around the world.

The first sod was turned at Alice Springs Station in July 2001 on an unusually wet day. The Ghan stood by the platform in all its glory, complete with the historic chairman's car attached. John Howard's smile reflecting his personal delight and commitment to the project.

At long last the economically defensible, freight expansionary, tourism enhancing, defence enabling, greenhouse friendly, culturally desirable and gauge sensible project was on its way to Darwin. Above all else, a long ago commitment given in federal legislation of 1911 was being honoured, which, it has to be said, in this age of cynicism about politics is important.

CHAPTER FOUR
RECORD BREAKING CONSTRUCTION

One hot Sunday afternoon in October 2002, I attended a very lively 90th anniversary service for Frontier Services (formerly the Inland Mission) in the centre of Alice Springs. I had some time to kill before a supper function so with thoughts of Flynn of the Inland and his pioneering work in the area, I decided to go for a walk. I gathered up my mobile phone, a water bottle, Akubra hat and camera and wandered to the Darwin end of the Alice Springs railway station. I was determined to do my own survey of the track work out of Alice Springs, which as it happened had begun one week before.

On a small 'boys own' type adventure, I began walking north, past some noisy trail bike riders until I was on my own. I reflected on the vision of Territorians such as Reverends John Flynn and Frank Rolland MC, who both argued for the railway, along with Eddie Connellan of Connellan Airways fame and Valben Louis Solomon. Solomon, a long-serving South Australian parliamentarian from Darwin and one of Darwin's first newspaper editors, made speech after speech in support of the railway project. More recently former Northern Territory Chief Minister Shane Stone and senators Bob Collins, Bernie Kilgariff and Grant Tambling added their enduring support. These good Territorians had a right to be very proud of the fact that the railway was happening at long last. Explorer John

McDouall Stuart and post-master general Sir Charles Todd also deserve to be saluted for their trail-blazing efforts in opening up the corridor from Adelaide to Darwin through Alice Springs in the mid 19th century.

I was standing somewhere west of the Stuart Highway, in the Todd River basin. I climbed up the single blade-width track into an ancient part of the MacDonnell Ranges. The deep blue of the distant hills and mountains contrasted with strips of bright reds and greys of the immediate landscape. My general direction remained north by north-west and I smiled to myself as I recalled two well-known railway-related movies of similar nomenclature, *North West Frontier* and *North by North-West*.

North West Frontier followed the fortunes of a group retreating from a tribal uprising by steam train. Filmed on location, including the mighty Khyber Pass, Kenneth Moore was at his best as he rescued distressed damsels and turned back attacks on the train. *North by North-West* featured both Cary Grant and the famous Twentieth Century Limited, the luxurious overnight train that ran between New York and Chicago via Albany from 1902 to 1967. The intrigue and deception of this film is something the operator of the Adelaide to Darwin Ghan will, no doubt, not want replicated on their train.

At last I reached a knoll that was about to be cut in half to allow the track to climb steadily out of the Alice Springs to Barrow Creek. Away in the distance to the south could be glimpsed Heavitree Gap, which forms both a natural channel for the Todd River and a path of travel used long before European settlement.

As I walked along I encountered, fluttering in the light breeze, bright pink tape pointing the way for the graders, not unlike the prayer flags found along trekking routes in Bhutan and Nepal. It was for me, as it always is in the gigantic wilderness of the MacDonnell Ranges, a solitary spiritual moment.

Enjoying the scenery, I plunged into the low scrub looking for the cross-over point of the Larapinta trail, the splendid walking track that leads out to the West MacDonnells and Simpson's Gap, Mount

Sonder and Mount Giles, to realise that I wasn't hallucinating in the mid-afternoon heat, but that I was completely lost, with a dead mobile phone battery and very little water. In the space of just one hour I had gone from a state of relaxed confidence to a degree of concern, and then real worry, as I stumbled around looking for markers. I did know I could always walk due south and eventually back into Alice Springs but it would be very late and dark by the time I arrived.

Suddenly a jeep surged over a sandhill and a group on a Sunday scrub bash asked if I would like a lift. Quick as a flash I jumped in before they changed their minds, or they realised I had once been deputy prime minister and it might be fun to make me walk an extra ten kilometres into town. Kindly they dropped me off at the Old Telegraph Station and, after a big iced coffee, I walked down the empty Todd River back into town and my supper function just in time.

The people of Alice Springs were very enthusiastic about the railway, even allowing for the fact that the town would lose some of its role as a transport hub. The advantages for the Territory and Australia dominated their decision to support the project, a positive and pleasant change from the often narrow and parochial thinking that too often emerges in Australian politics.

So, when not one blade of grass nor one metre of dirt had been moved in Alice Springs twelve months after the turning of the first sod, locals were beginning to think nothing was ever going to happen. This was, after all, where work had been suspended and then ended by the Hawke/Keating government after its election in 1983. However, this time it was all about keeping to a grand plan that saw work commence further north, initially at Katherine and Tennant Creek.

The reason given for this strategy was to take account of the Territory's wet and dry seasons, by expediting construction during the dry and thus avoiding the extraordinary floods and giant quagmires of the wet. However, the cynic might take the view that once the central section from Tennant Creek to north of Katherine was in place, neither the bankers nor the politicians could change their minds and pull the plug on the project. The remaining two gaps in the track back down to Alice Springs and up to Darwin would stick out like the proverbial and it would be a matter of acute embarrassment to all if the rail was not completed.

On a more practical level, the creation of not one but two sleeper factories, one at Tennant Creek and the other at Katherine, reduced the costs of transporting the two million concrete sleepers required and helped boost decentralisation in the Territory, at least for a period. These two giant sleeper factories in the middle of the outback set a cracking production pace. Tennant Creek was the larger factory with a capacity of 2400 sleepers a day, while Katherine produced some 1600 a day. However, both plants often exceeded production targets. In a symbolic north–south connection the diamond saws used by the sleeper factories were supplied by a joint venture of four small businesses located in the Iron Triangle at Whyalla.[1]

Of course, a much bigger contract was for 144 000 tonnes of steel rail needed for the project and this was won by another Whyalla company, Whyalla One Steel, previously owned by BHP. By the middle of 2002 some 60 000 tonnes of rail had already been rolled and moved by special train to the cattle yards at Roe Creek just south of Alice Springs and then by purpose built road trains up the track. The steel rail had to be specially canted as a result of the sleeper shape, and held under compression to withstand heat expansion and cold contraction. If the rail had not been so engineered then there would have been over a kilometre difference between the point of greatest contraction and the point of greatest expansion.

In addition to the two million sleepers and 144 000 tonnes of rail,

---

1. Action Engineering Industries, Marand Precision and Northern Scaffolding teamed together and with assistance from Whyalla Fabrications delivered this vital apparatus.

nearly 100 bridges and 1500 culverts were needed and all with the capacity to handle a 1 in a 100 year flood.

Over 8 million pandrol clips (which have replaced rail spikes), made in Blacktown Sydney, hold the rails in place on their concrete sleepers and ballast bed. So there are another 8 million reasons why during long periods of extreme heat, the rails will not suddenly expand across the Timor Sea towards Indonesia. This might just be enough to satisfy the 'anti Australian brigade' in Jakarta that the project is not some form of subtle aggression by Australia towards its huge neighbour! The 'rail to Asia' project aims in reality to do the very opposite. It is all about building a two-way relationship and encouraging trade in both directions. The South Australian government created a unit with this name within its Department of Industry and Trade to do just this.

Clare Forrest, a very distant relation of Sir John Forrest, was one of the many 'doing the hard yards' out along the track. Working in the searing heat as site clerk at the construction camps, she travelled with the construction teams as they moved along the route laying track. She spent some time at Sandover Camp, just north of where I stumbled around along the Great Larapinta Grade.

Fighting sweat and flies, the construction teams graded the earth base allowing the giant track-laying machine to move forward to accurately place the sleepers and then the heavy rails and clips. After welding the rail, ballast ore trains then moved through for the final tamping of the track.

Temperatures varied from 46° Celsius to −2° Celsius with desert wind blasts adding to the discomfort. Some 150 construction crew worked with determination and pride month in and month out. Covering many areas of skill, crews comprised surveyors, environmental officers, bus drivers, machine operators, fitters and boilermakers, labourers, caterers, cleaners and team managers.

One of Clare Forrest's duties was to help organise social and recreational activities for her crew. There were night cricket and golf games, even athletic events bearing the banner of the Greek Olympics! All of these attempts to build morale in these incredibly difficult conditions were replicated by the other construction teams as they worked to stay ahead of schedule and for their place in the history.

Men greatly outnumbered women in the project workforce but there were more women ready to do it tough than might be expected. They worked as water cart operators, scrapers and bulldozer drivers. And Darwin's first Great Southern Railway station master, Debra Parker, is a woman with years of rail experience under her belt.

The workforce was drawn from all over Australia, and was of all ages. As one surfie from Sydney's beaches remarked, it is a long time between waves but worth it for the money and the chance to be involved in the project. And, as with many of Australia's big engineering projects such as the O'Connor pipeline from Perth to Kalgoorlie and the massive Snowy Mountains Scheme of the 1950s and 1960s, a number of migrants from Poland and other parts of eastern Europe were attracted to the Adelaide–Darwin railway, anxious to get a start in their new country. These first generation Australians may have been distant relatives of the hundreds who flocked to the Snowy scheme five decades before. They were joined by well over 100 Aboriginal workers who came from all parts of the Northern Territory. It is to be hoped that this dedicated and huge workforce will be recognised again and thanked well into the future in the same way the Snowy workers were.

As the 2003 wet season ran out of puff in Australia's Top End, track laying recommenced towards Darwin from Katherine. The formation earthworks completed before the wet survived the months of torrential rain without breaking down. Crater Lake cutting, the biggest cutting of them all at a depth of 33 metres, was sliced straight through a ridge of colourful rock and its steep walls were as clean as the day they were cut when I sighted them in all their glory at dawn on 4 April 2003. The cutting was at peace ahead of the noise of the track-laying operations.

The good news is that The Ghan passenger train travels through this spectacular section from Katherine to Darwin during daylight hours in both directions. This also allows passengers to sight the Fergusson River bridge, built in 1918 and now the world's only major railway bridge where the rail track has been switched from narrow to standard gauge. At a length of 128 metres, the Fergusson River bridge rightly deserves the title 'the greatest recycled railway bridge in the world'.

There are three longer bridges along the railway: the Elizabeth River bridge over a tidal estuary near the terminus at Darwin at 510 metres, the Katherine River bridge at 240 metres and the Adelaide River bridge at 150 metres. All three were completed early and efficiently and well ahead of the track-laying operation. However, Murphy's Law took over when a team from ABC-TV's *New Dimensions* turned up to film the rail being laid over the Adelaide River bridge in July 2003. Some guide sensors on the huge ADrail track-laying machine broke off at the critical moment bringing the otherwise smooth operation to a halt. The subsequent program went to air on 28 August 2003 and helped boost interest in the project.

With the wet out of the way, the planning engineers of ADrail began locking in dates for the completion, handover and commencement of operations. They did this in the knowledge that Australia's second transcontinental railway had gathered an outstanding workforce which had completed laying the track well ahead of schedule. The project completion date was regularly brought forward despite setbacks such as a train derailment and a tragic death at a level-crossing accident.

In an eerie repeat of circumstances surrounding Australia's first transcontinental railway, the second transcontinental was also finished during a time of world conflict. But this time it was a war against terrorism. The horrific railway bombings in Moscow and Madrid in early 2004, which killed hundreds of innocent people, and the bomb threats against the French Railways are a potent reminder of the troubled times in which we live. Equally, the successful completion of the world's newest transcontinental is something to be celebrated.

In September 2003, nine months ahead of schedule and perversely 90 years late, the final welding of rails took place in brilliant sunshine just on the edge of Alice Springs. The champagne-free ceremony was brief and the crowd small, but it was certainly easy to get three cheers for the world's newest transcontinental railway and those who had built it.

The South Australian premier, Mike Rann, reminded the gathering of a proposal that once existed to name South Australia and the Northern Territory Albert State, and I read a poem I had written about Mark Twain and his train journey Down Under.

> In 1896 the America author Mark Twain
> Came to Australia and caught the Sydney–Melbourne train.
> Suddenly at dawn the cry went up 'All Passengers Change'.
> This is the oddest thing, cursed Mark Twain
> As the train reached Albury and break of gauge pain.
> He asked, 'Which idiot legislator dreamt up this change?'
> It took decades to fix, 22 gauges remiss.
> Now today Mark Twain would be able to say
> 'Job well done, as at long last you can travel by train,
> without break of gauge strain'.

I also reminded the gathering of the famous telegram sent from Promontory, Utah, when the first transcontinental railway was completed in the United States. It simply read: 'Done'.

One week later, during a brilliant dawn ceremony at East Arm, Darwin's new port, plaques were unveiled to celebrate the end of the construction phase. A bright red sun rose on cue.

Before the formal ceremony began I produced a golden tape measure and double-checked the gauge. It was spot on the 1435 mm of Stephenson's standard. The Northern Territory Chief Minister,

Claire Martin, remarked that it seemed I was fixated by gauge. She was probably right, but it was worth making that one cheeky check.

The final pandrol clips were driven into place, presumably numbers 7 999 999 and 8 000 000. The first Lord Mayor of Darwin, Dr Ella Stack, then produced the original clip made when the standard gauge first entered the Northern Territory in 1979.

At long last the signals for the world's newest transcontinental were all green. All that was now needed was intensive track testing before operations began in early 2004.

CHAPTER FIVE
AUSTRALIA REVAMPS RAIL

No one will ever know how close the railways of Australia came to total collapse in the last half of the 20th century. In this realm with its state-based fiefdoms, there was no great 'Beeching bombshell' as was the case in Great Britain in the 1960s when Lord Richard Beeching identified hundreds of stations, branch lines, and link lines for closure. (In fairness to Beeching, he pointed a way ahead for rail in the United Kingdom.) Rather, Australia's railways faced death by a thousand cuts, that is, expenditure cuts. There was little new capital investment on track upgrades, overheads were huge, there was chronic overstaffing and, worse still, rail tried to be everything to everybody.

In 1997, after various studies, Professor Philip Laird confirmed that Australia had hit the bottom of the barrel. For a country with an extensive operational railway network, we still managed to have the highest road freight usage per capita in the world, while the cost of road accidents in 1993 was an estimated $14 980 million. Up until that year rail accidents, on the other hand, had cost Australia $69 million, aviation accidents $75 million and maritime accidents $316 million.

As luck would have it, a number of factors helped rail struggle through this period. The advent of large-scale coal mining operations in New South Wales and Queensland saw major rail development to handle the transport of millions of tonnes of coal using bulk balloon loops. This configuration allowed trains to load and unload while continuing to move forward in one direction. Containerisation of freight from 1960 onwards also boosted the chances of rail by providing a pilfer-proof long haul alternative to road freight. Western Australia rail was helped by a massive expansion in both the mineral sands and bauxite mining industries, as well as huge growth in the grain-growing industries. However, it was bulk iron ore requirements in the Pilbara region that saw two new railways built from the inland to Dampier and Port Hedland in the 1960s.

Against the odds, a team led by GW Hills raced to get the Hamersley railway built in time for the first shipments of iron ore from Dampier. On 2 April 1966, a severe cyclone named 'Shirley' crossed the coast at Dampier and dumped 175 mm of rain over a couple of hours. Bridges and embankments collapsed at eighteen different locations. All had to be rebuilt within one month. Today, the world's leading heavy haulage bulk railways operate in the Pilbara.

The introduction of the mighty diesel and diesel-electric locomotive in the first two decades after World War II boosted efficiency and speeded up timetables. This was due to their faster acceleration and quicker turn-around times when compared to the beautiful but inefficient and generally less powerful steam locomotives.

However, the most decisive intervention in improving freight and long-distance passenger rail in Australia can be credited to the colourful WC Wentworth, MP.

Born in 1907, Bill Wentworth had a habit of causing upsets during his long public life. (On a World War II exercise on Sydney's Botany Bay, his small unit managed to capture half of the city and greatly embarrass the generals of the day.) In 1949, he entered the federal parliament for the Liberal Party, representing the northern Sydney seat of Mackellar. He never really got on with Liberal leader and prime minister, RG Menzies.

A great reader, Bill Wentworth cared little about appearance and more about the big issues of the day. Former Transport minister Ralph Hunt recalls Bill arriving at outback Narrabri by plane having left his coat behind. On closer inspection he was found to be wearing one black shoe and one brown shoe!

Bill Wentworth chaired and drove the parliamentary committee that produced the Wentworth Report in 1956, which recommended standardising the railways, including the important Sydney to Melbourne route. However, this recommendation wasn't universally accepted. Many people in my old seat of Farrer saw the standard gauge as an economic threat, predicting massive job losses as a result of both freight and passenger trains no longer having to stop at the Albury-Wodonga junction.

As well as the Sydney to Melbourne route, the report recommended standardising Broken Hill to Port Pirie and Adelaide, as well as Kalgoorlie to Perth. Significantly, it ruled out the wholesale and costly standardisation of the entire Victorian and South Australian systems, a project that would never have received the Treasurer's blessing. It also pushed for a dual gauge (narrow/standard) track from Mount Isa to Townsville, highlighting the fact that the giant Burdekin River bridge between Charters Towers and Townsville already provided for a dual gauge operation.

The Wentworth Report quickly became a prod to the federal and state governments to improve the efficiency of the national rail networks. However, it was not until 2 January 1962 that the first through train, wisely a freight train, departed Sydney for Melbourne.

The Southern Aurora, a new and modestly luxurious express sleeper train between Melbourne and Sydney, also commenced running that year, but poor old Bill Wentworth was not on the inaugural trip. So his firebrand wife, Barbara, held up a placard as the train left Sydney's Central Station with the simple message, 'Where is Bill W?'. Unfortunately, parliament was sitting and Bill could not get a pair to cover his leave of absence. When the House of Representatives eventually adjourned that night, Bill made a dash out of Canberra by car to join the inaugural Southern Aurora in the middle of the night and at the halfway mark!

Nearly 100 years after the first train services began running between Sydney and Melbourne, passengers could now sleep all the way through without having to change trains. The Southern Aurora also had a dining car and lounge car of adequate luxury but there was no piano on board as the journey was considered too short. The Spirit of Progress backed up the Southern Aurora as an overnight service with sitting cars only, while the Intercapital Daylight express offered a thirteen hour service and a buffet car of renown. There may have been no kippers or caviar, but it was certainly better than the microwave-dominated snack bars on many trains today.

The amount of freight going by rail improved slightly on this Sydney–Melbourne corridor, but it remained at well below 20 per cent of total freight movements, unlike the Nullarbor where over 75 per cent of freight is now going by rail.

Albury-Wodonga did not lose out. While the number of rail jobs were greatly reduced, the twin cities attracted major decentralisation projects such as Uncle Ben's Pet Foods and the large Australian Newsprint Mills' papermill. In mid-2003 the giant retailer Woolworths announced a major national distribution centre, with its own standard gauge railway sidings, to be built just west of Albury-Wodonga.

What went wrong? Why did rail fail to capture the many opportunities created by standardisation?

The answer rests with the fact that each state's rail system operated as a fiefdom. Rail has also never had a strong lobby, and has always played second fiddle to the powerful road transport lobby. There were few ministers at state or federal level who understood the need for a balance between road and rail and that both should operate together and not in competition. Some very tough decisions needed to be taken, but governments were often easily tilted by their transport departments and road authorities to support road priorities over rail. Every step forward for the railways of Australia between 1945 and 1995 was matched by at least one counter-step of one kind or another.

Witness the opening of the Sydney–Melbourne standard gauge link in 1962. Every train running straight through, in fact, had to stop at Albury for fifteen to twenty minutes so the locomotives and crews could be changed, the brake pressure system could be checked and all of the axles checked manually.

It was a ridiculous late night scene at Albury station as the north-bound Spirit of Progress crept slowly into the platform so each axle could be tested by two men with torches. (Today this is done auto-matically by trackside machines. The system is so finely tuned that the drivers in the locomotive cabin know of trouble and bearing overheating at the same time as the train operators.) When the all clear was given, the Spirit of Progress would glide out of the plat-form heading to Sydney ahead of the northbound Southern Aurora, which would then be put through the same tedious routine. This would happen six times a day to each of the supposed through passenger trains. Compounding the problem was the absurd decision to use rail in building the new track from Wodonga to Spencer Street, Melbourne that was lighter than the rail used on the New South Wales side. This caused different axle weight allowances in freight train loading.

It took decades for some of these absurdities to be fixed, not only at Albury but also at break of gauge points and the fiefdom bound-aries at Broken Hill and Port Pirie, Kalgoorlie and nearby Parkeston. Some of the overstaffing problems remain to this day.

A case in point is Medway Junction, between Marulan and Wingello on the busy Sydney–Goulburn main line. A couple of trains a day make their way to and from the Marulan South Limestone Quarry through this tiny junction. In a long overdue move, it was decided to install modern equipment that would allow the junction to be operated from the large Goulburn signal box. Some two to three jobs would be lost at the junction, but job opportunities existed in nearby Goulburn. There was also the danger that the quarry owner, Boral, would switch to road if rail freight was not competitive.

As detailed in *Railway Digest*, the cutover day was scheduled for mid December 2002, but it was not to be. An extraordinary order came from above that the modern switching equipment was to be left switched off and that Medway Junction would continue to be manned locally. As I drove into the awe-inspiring Long Point Lookout just past the tiny Medway Junction box in early 2003, I found this was definitely the case. I smiled to myself and thought how far rail had come, yet how far it still had to go! (The cutover was eventually made in 2004.)

Nevertheless at the beginning of the 21st century Australia is starting to revamp rail in a significant way, learning, sometimes the hard way, that there can be too much penny pinching.

Queensland Rail began the new century by discovering how even the smallest component, worth just a few cents, can cause havoc. As a coal train made its way down a steep escarpment into Hay Point, south of Mackay, this cheap component failed forcing the driver in the lead locomotive to lose control when the middle locos accelerated instead of braking. The train, in fact, accelerated over the outside track, plunging down the slope. Fortunately, no one was killed but a few more dollars spent on a back-up system would have stopped a potential tragedy and saved many thousands of dollars, the cost of cleaning up the derailment.

Competition, not only with road but also within rail, has driven the revamp. Freight from Melbourne to Perth, for example, can be sent by one of two operators and five freight forwarders. The rail operators can decide to provide their own trains and locomotives or choose to outsource. When outsourcing, freight forwarders such as FCL load their wagons, often double stacking, taking them to a departure track. Freight Australia or Pacific National will then turn up with their locomotives and hook and haul to destination.

Out of frustration with the deplorable track between Brisbane, Sydney and Melbourne Chris Corrigan of Patricks, who with Paul Little of Toll formed Pacific National, spent part of 2003 lashing out at the rail priorities of the nation. He complained that the rail project to Darwin would be as useful as testicles on a tick.

This creative climate has resulted in some interesting developments such as with Specialized Container Transport Ltd in Altona, Victoria, which has cleverly positioned itself to win back pallet freight for rail by utilising computers to ensure old-style box cars with high-speed new bogies are packed evenly and to the brim. These box cars are able to be precision refrigerated and so in the lead-up to Easter each year hundreds of pallets of Easter eggs can be sent safely and swiftly across the Nullarbor Plain by rail. Also at Altona, Colin Rees Transport Ltd (CRT) has imported German equipment to develop the cargo sprinter concept in Australia. This allows short haul, small loads of containers to be moved efficiently and is very suitable for regional branch lines.

Bulk freight, such as grain, coal and iron ore, is tailor-made for rail. Unfortunately, slow load out and unload facilities and the inadequate provision of balloon loops means that rail freight isn't always efficient. Nevertheless, the chances for bulk freight were boosted on 1 July 2000 when rail diesel fuel excise tax was abolished and with investment in state-of-the-art bulk rail wagons.

Bradken Rail at Ipswich in Queensland and Mittagong in New South Wales is building new-style freight wagons along with EDI, previously Clyde Engineering. The hazards of decentralisation became very clear for Bradken in the firestorm summer of 2002–2003 when a fast fire swept to within a couple of metres of its Mittagong plant. The accusation was often made in the past that steam trains started many fires. This is not the case today, as steam trains are not allowed to operate on days of a total fire ban in most jurisdictions.

Big harvest years are always a huge boost for rail revenue as bulk freight is the best way to transport grain. However, it was not that long ago that all the wagons at the huge Geelong grain terminal had to be shovelled and swept out manually. Bulk bottom-dumping wagons have now been widely introduced. Unfortunately, grain farming is fickle, so while ARG in Western Australia enjoyed a record 12 million tonne plus grain harvest in 2003, the eastern rail operators had to contend with slim pickings from a small drought harvest in New South Wales and Victoria.

Mercifully, rail is just about out of parcel freight unless it has been consolidated into containers. Sydney to Perth mail, for example, is loaded by Australia Post into large B-double road trucks in the afternoon. These move swiftly overnight across the Great Dividing Range to Parkes, where Bill Gibbons of FCL has built an intermodal depot, just to the west at Goobang Junction. Around dawn, the containers are loaded onto a double-stacked freight train that runs directly to Perth, cutting one day off the previous schedule.

The big private rail freight operators are hungry for business. These operators now include Freight Australia with headquarters in Melbourne, Pacific National with headquarters at Sydney, Perth-based ARG, and several others including the tiny Tasrail headquartered in Launceston. Do not underestimate Tasrail: it has made a profit in each of the five years since it was sold by the Tasmanian government, not bad after the previous 100 years of losses! The demand by private rail for lean, efficient and very commercial operations is a far cry from the railway culture that existed under public ownership when too often the customer came last. The success of private rail freight has even impacted on the mighty government-owned Queensland Railways, which now carries over 150 million tonnes of freight each year.

While rail freight has gathered traction, the passenger business is another matter. Heavy subsidies are required to maintain both the suburban and regional commuter services, partly as motor vehicle usage has been under-taxed, particularly during peak periods. Brisbane, Sydney, Melbourne and Perth all have electric suburban train networks and all have been extended in recent years. However, all these cities also need central zones where cars are required to pay an automatic toll for entry and a higher toll during peak periods. London and Singapore currently do this and both have very extensive suburban rail systems, in fact, Singapore has arguably the best metro in the world.

The main Singapore network, or SMRT, was the first subway system to be built with passenger protection doors. Each weekday the SMRT, which continues to expand, carries over 1.1 million passengers. Train punctuality is at over 95 per cent while the ultra-modern fare ticketing system, provided by an Australian company, ran at a profit of some $72 million for the year ending 31 March 2003.

Many quaint features remain with Australia's suburban and regional railways including no electrification in Adelaide. In Brisbane, despite the fact that the rail track runs directly alongside the upgraded Lang Park football stadium, the stadium rail platform is further away than the carpark. In Sydney trains using the Carlingford line are banished from the City Circle as they cause too many point changes at their junction with the main western line at Clyde if they run through. Melbourne ripped up the outer circle plans, letting go the key railway easements. It also ripped up a unique Irish broad light rail tram line (all of Melbourne's other tram lines were built to standard gauge) that ran from Brighton along the beaches through Sandringham to Beaumaris. For the record, Melbourne comes third for length of tram track (238 kilometres), behind St Petersburg (344 track kilometres) and Katowice (245 kilometres) but ahead of Sofia (222 kilometres) and mighty Moscow (220 kilometres).

Some sentimentality exists around Australian trains, particularly commuter trains, such as 'The Fish' and 'The Chips' which run on Sydney's Blue Mountains line. For a time, there was also 'The Heron' running from Emu Plains to Central, but thankfully no 'Sting Ray'! More recently 'The River' commenced operation to connect Sydney's western suburbs to the Central Coast. With a renewed emphasis on inner city living, more circle routes will be needed to keep up with passenger demand, as well as automatic ticket systems that actually work and can be easily policed.

A particularly extraordinary dimension of the Sydney suburban system is the use of double-decker cars. In the early 1960s, Sydney was enjoying strong economic growth and the suburban system was heavily overcrowded. The existing suburban fleet had manual doors, which were often kept open between stops to assist ventilation during Sydney's heavily humid summers.

In 1962 and 1963 when the New South Wales Railways and its famous commissioner, Neal McCusker, began thinking about introducing power-operated centrally controlled doors to the existing carriages, an engineer named Roy Leembruggen asked two very simple questions: why not develop double-decker trains to ease crowding and why not build into the new cars power-operated doors? New South Wales Railways was quickly persuaded and tenders were called for the first-ever double-decker suburban train carriage.

The brilliant vision of Dr JJC Bradfield then came into play. His famous Sydney Harbour Bridge had been designed and built to cater for the high clearance required for United States-style electric trains, including at the critical approach tunnels and pylons. Bradfield had succeeded in laying down an above rail height of 14' 6" for Sydney's electric trains, which was a vital 6" higher than that used for most Australian country main lines, and well over 2' higher and much wider than the restrictive British loading gauge which continues to this day. This allowed Roy Leembruggen and his small team to draft working drawings of two level carriages with a generous internal 6' 3" head clearance.

In Britain in 1949, British Southern Railway produced two prototype four-car double-deckers that ran on the third rail electric system from London to Gravesend. They proved not to be a success and the only UK4DD units built vanished from service completely.

Leembruggen's new double-deckers were built and put into operation between 1964 and 1968. An eight-car, all double-decker configuration meant a 1900 passenger capacity compared to 1000 previously. This huge expansion in peak hour capability was achieved without having to undertake expensive track duplication. Railway planners around the world soon became very interested in Sydney's first generation double-deckers. In what must be described as naiveté in the extreme, copies of the working drawings were made available free of charge to SNCF France, DB Germany and eight other systems. There was a railway version of Santa Claus after all. Today, the intellectual property and detailed design work would have been sold for millions of dollars.

When the world hall of fame for railway engineers is developed as part of the 200-year celebration of rail, there has to be a place for Saint Roy Leembruggen as creator and patron saint of the overhead, electric-driven, full-length, double-decker trains. He will be deservedly near the top of the list. Meanwhile this boy from Strathfield lives quietly up the North Shore line in Sydney, reflecting not so much on what might have been but on what is yet still to be designed to boost rail.

Sydney remains the only significant operator of double-decker suburban and regional services in the southern hemisphere. In fact, except for a couple of stray carriages and one early four-car set on the Melbourne system, it is the only operator of double-decker carriages south of the equator. The double-decker has helped underpin rapid passenger growth in Sydney, including for major events such as the Sydney Olympics and the massive annual Royal Easter Show at Homebush.

Passenger levels are growing beyond Sydney. This is particularly so for skilful operators such as the Great Southern Railway which owns and operates both the north–south Ghan and the east–west Indian Pacific as well as the Overland between Adelaide and Melbourne. The Ghan and the Indian Pacific are making a profit but the Overland struggles, except of course when one of the Adelaide football teams is in an AFL final at the Melbourne Cricket Ground, then the Overland runs at record length, loaded up with fans.

In twenty years of service, New South Wales' XPT has been barely competitive. Is is, however, more economical than the Victorian approach, which in the 21st century still involves a large locomotive hauling tiny three-car passenger train sets in a costly mismatch. The Sydney to Broken Hill Explorer service completes some sections out west at speeds exceeding 140 kph, but has to crawl at 40 kph over the tight curves and grades of the Blue Mountains.

In Queensland, revenues from over 150 million tonnes of coal freight annually allow some cross subsidy of passenger services. Queensland Rail has the most diverse range of rolling stock from fast-tilt trains to the very slow Inlander. Then there was the indulgent luxury of the Great South Pacific Express, operated for a few years from the late 1990s in conjunction with the Oriental Express Company. Starting at Kuranda, on the range just north of Cairns, it ran to Brisbane and, with bogie change further south, it would travel to the Hunter Valley and Sydney from time to time.

My wife Judy and I travelled with the premier of Queensland, Peter Beattie, and a host of VIPs on the inaugural journey. It was a luxurious experience, but alas federal cabinet commitments down south meant having to leave the train early on the second day. Not even my well-honed scheduling skills could alter that personal disaster. In March 2003 it was announced that this service would cease operations, a victim of the downturn in tourism in part caused by the second Gulf War and the SARS plague. The carriages were last sighted peacefully at rest at the magnificent Ipswich Railway Workshop Museum.

Western Australia is revamping the Prospector, its Perth to Kalgoorlie service, and runs two other country trains, one a commuter service to Northam, the other The Australind to Albany. One very hot Sunday I departed Perth on the Prospector with strict instructions from the local state member Max Trenorden to get off at the wayside stop of Grass Valley. The train was comfortable and very cool. It stopped right on time. The conductor asked if I was sure about this. There was nobody to be seen waiting for me in the fierce heat at Grass Valley. With some reluctance and a sense of foreboding I waved goodbye to the train and waited in the shade of a steel wheat silo thinking what I would do to Max if and when he turned up. Five minutes later a car emerged from behind a distant wheat storage shed and rolled along to the siding. Out jumped Max with an evil smile to tell me he thought he would give me a test of faith! It took a number of very cold beers and several years to overcome this bit of fun at my expense.

Other than interstate trains, South Australia has no country passenger trains. However, it did discover the value of rail tourism and started a regular tourist train from Adelaide to the Barossa Valley, famous for its wines, gourmet food and spas. Sadly, this service was unsuccessful, despite Queen Elizabeth II giving it a go in 2002. There is talk of an exciting project to the McLaren Valley, one hour south of Adelaide. The idea is to install a Suez Walhalla Whitfield narrow gauge operation on an old broad gauge easement. This would allow a bike track to be combined with a tourist rail. This will take some time to develop and require a considerable amount of fund raising.

Until recently Tasmania had no regular modern passenger rail services beyond some charter tourist trains operated by Don River Rail, at New Norfolk near Hobart and at Port Arthur. In early 2003 the Abt Railway was finally re-opened from Queenstown to Strahan. Over $20 million from the federal Federation Fund was poured into this worthwhile project, the only rack and pinion narrow gauge railway in Australia, Mount Morgan near Rockhampton having been long since closed. The Abt Railway, with its very steep grade, is an exciting and very picturesque trip, and has a jewel of a station at Queenstown. Steam Tasmania has also started a special service, travelling over most of the island's disused track through abundant and superb scenery.

Many of the entirely tourist train operations around Australia provide wonderful journeys. Pichi Richi from Quorn to Port Augusta is by far the most historic and noble, while the Goolwa to Port Elliot railway, Australia's first ever public railway, celebrated its 150th anniversary in 2004. The Walhalla Gold Railway runs from Walhalla in Gippsland to Thompson River and, it is hoped soon again, to Erica. Reopened in 2002, it provided a great community service one week later when a landslide closed the only road into the tiny heritage village of Walhalla. The Puffing Billy is the biggest tourist train of them all and connects directly with the Melbourne to Belgrave electric train service. There are many more successful tourist train trips such as the Hotham Valley and Carnarvon Wharf in the west, and the totally isolated Gulflander from Normanton to Croydon in the north.

There have, however, been some absolute disasters, such as the Dorrigo to Glenreagh service in New South Wales. In a classic case of disunity is death, several decades of fights over priorities and ownership led to its failure. If anyone can remember, the project was supposed to have provided for both a museum at Dorrigo and for trains to run from Glenreagh on the north coast main line (north of Coffs Harbour) up the magnificent escarpment through two tunnels to Dorrigo on top of the Great Dividing Range. Gradually, a determined effort by many is seeing the project put back on track. Meanwhile, a huge collection of steam locomotives remains at rest in the Dorrigo rail yards.

In New South Wales the famous Zig Zag Heritage Railway on the western side of the Blue Mountains is one of the best of them all, utilising as it does the Whitton Pathway from Mount Victoria down to the valley floor and Lithgow. (John Whitton was New South Wales Railway's engineer-in-chief from 1857 to 1890. He set high standards throughout his tenure.) The two zig zags were brilliantly engineered over 100 years ago, and the sandstone bridges still do a sterling job today. The Zig Zag Railway was converted from standard gauge to Anglo Cape narrow gauge in 1975. As a result, most of its rolling stock is from Queensland. A bizarre consequence of this is that, at the start of the 21st century, the only gauge that can be said to be operating in all six states of Australia is the Anglo Cape narrow gauge!

What has emerged in Australia is that properly operated tourist trains, either on dedicated and often narrow gauge tracks or as charter services on existing operational tracks (such as the Cockatoo Run up the escarpment from Wollongong to Moss Vale in New South Wales), can work well and generate profits. The key to success is a regular, reliable schedule, including during summer and total fireban days when steam has to be replaced by diesel.

New Zealand has also gone through a century of network contraction on its extensive Anglo Cape narrow gauge system, on both the North and South islands. Once again familiar mistakes were made in the very early days with Irish broad gauge being adopted for the Christchurch area, while standard gauge was laid out in both Auckland in the North Island and Invercargill at the tip of the South Island. Elsewhere Anglo Cape gauge became the norm. This was particularly so for short-haul tracks from the hinterland to the nearest port.

Eventually, and much earlier than in Australia, wisdom prevailed with the arrival of the far-sighted Sir Julius Vogel. As carefully recorded by Geoffrey Churchman and Tony Hurst in their history of the railways of New Zealand, Vogel became colonial treasurer in 1869 and spearheaded expansion of the New Zealand railways. The sensible and narrow Anglo Cape gauge became the national standard gauge. Vogel also ensured that the network was developed along national lines and not just as a series of short lines to port, so work commenced on the trunk lines from Auckland to Wellington on the North Island and from Picton to Invercargill on the east coast of the South Island. It was a mammoth task.

So unfolded a rapid expansion of the New Zealand rail network in the last quarter of the 19th century. A superb 140 km-long north-south line from Kingston near Queenstown to the port of Invercargill was completed in 1878. Sadly, only the northern and southernmost sections remain open today, the middle section having long since closed. A delightful tourist steam train departs Kingston during the summer months for a great run south, but as is often the case, there is no longer a connection to the ferry from Queenstown, so this tourist train operation struggles along.

After I stepped down as minister for trade, I attended an APEC-related conference in Queenstown as a government envoy. I was able to arrange a quick trip by car from Queenstown, a spectacular city on Lake Wakatipu, to Kingston. At Kingston, the steam locomotive was nestled alongside the lake ready to go. We were soon hurtling south, climbing out of Kingston over a small saddle but surrounded by giant snow-capped mountains on either side.

On completion of the southbound run, the locomotive disconnected from the carriages and whipped around a triangle to face the correct direction to steam back up the valley to Kingston. Being able to travel in the vintage rolling stock of the 'Kingston Flyer' was a joy, particularly as it was very well maintained. It was a refreshing interlude after the conference had finished and it was good to see New Zealand hanging on to part of its rail heritage.

I dashed back to Queenstown airport and caught an early afternoon flight directly from Queenstown to Sydney and then on to Wagga Wagga. I remember walking in the back door of Peppers, the farm at Boree Creek, just before sunset having started the day at dawn in Queenstown, New Zealand, thinking you can pack a lot into one day, particularly with careful planning.

Over the decades the railways of New Zealand experienced stop-start support as the financial circumstances of the New Zealand government waxed and waned and priorities changed. The last big project in the 20th century, ahead of the controversial privatisation of the railway in 1999, was the electrification of 412 kilometres along the North Island trunk line between Auckland, the original capital, and Wellington, the current capital of New Zealand. This project included electrification of the famous Raurimu Spiral where the North Island Main Trunk climbed over 200 metres in under six kilometres, utilising two tunnels to do so with the track crossing over itself to gain extra height.

Spiral track is a favourite tool of engineers in steep terrain, particularly in Canada and Switzerland. Even in relatively flat New South Wales, two spirals have been built, one at Bethungra on the Melbourne–Sydney main line, and the other just north of Kyogle near The Risk on the Sydney–Brisbane main line.

Electrification of the Auckland–Wellington main line was one of a list of projects brought forward by the controversial and fiercely conservative political leader, 'Piggy' Muldoon. As prime minister he decided to launch a number of big projects in order to win another term in the 1970s. Unfortunately, only a section of the main line was electrified, from Palmerston North to Hamilton but including the Raurimu spiral.

Piggy Muldoon's approach to rail was a bit like the advice he gave to new government backbenchers: you must be sincere, genuine and sympathetic at all times and, until you learn how to fake doing this, you will never succeed.

Despite a half-electrified main line, the Kiwis did make some good progress in running their rail services. Helped by the revenue from the ferries plying between the North and South islands, New Zealand's railways did make a profit in the last two years before privatisation. This financial success extended into the first two years under private control but by 2002, economic downturn affected profitability. Still, new freight services have been successfully introduced, such as the bulk milk service on the South Island, and the Christchurch to Greymouth Trans Alpine Express remains one of the most scenic day trips anywhere in the world. Travelling east–west across the South Island, it passes through plains, gorges and glaciers, and skirts rainforests and nearby mountain peaks covered in snow.

What project would leapfrog New Zealand railways into the future? This would have to be a tunnel or bridge linking the North and South islands by rail. However, this treacherous narrow channel is extremely deep, so a direct link is far too costly to contemplate. In the meantime the ferries do the job adequately.

All in all, by a combination of chance and commitment, the railway realm of Australia and nearby New Zealand has come alive as the 21st century unfolds. Passenger and freight rail is here to stay, some of it even profitably. New tracks are being built, extra services are being provided and even sentimental rail tourism is improving, overcoming huge insurance premium hikes along the way.

There is one last issue to settle, that is simply, where was the first railway built Down Under? It is clear the first public railway was the Goolwa–Port Elliot railway in South Australia which opened in 1854. In her excellent book, *Romance of Australian Railways*, Patsy Adam-Smith claims the first Australian railway was in Tasmania from Taranna to Oakwood, near the penal settlement of Port Arthur. The carriages were apparently operated by convicts running alongside and pushing on big handles. This unusual wooden rail project was devised by Captain O'Hara Booth and opened in 1836. On this occasion Patsy Adam-Smith is wrong.

The very first railway, public, private or penal, was in fact built in Newcastle near the mouth of the Hunter River by Australia's second oldest company, the Australian Agricultural Company, to haul coal. The standard gauge railway ran from Church Street, or Pit A, over Hunter Street to the wharf area, a distance of about 15 chains. It commenced operations in 1831 as a funicular railway but was a railed-way nevertheless. It was soon extended to serve adjoining pits and spread out over several kilometres.

In awarding this honour to Newcastle, I declare an interest as a director of the Australian Agricultural Company. The Newcastle Regional Public Library provides efficient confirmation of all of this, including the fact that Australia's first coal export went down this railway to be loaded in December 1831 on the *Sophia Jane* bound for India. The *Sophia Jane* was also the first steamship to visit Australia and in turn it might be able to claim credit for the invention of the antipodean version of the phrase 'Carrying coals to Newcastle'.

It has been a long journey Down Under for rail since 1831. Despite Australia's dubious world record of having 22 gauges, and still counting, the most exciting phase lies ahead in the 21st century.

PART TWO

GLOBAL RENAISSANCE

CHAPTER SIX

GREAT BRITAIN: THE BIRTHPLACE OF RAIL

Queen Victoria and Winston Churchill both had a great love of train travel. More recently Queen Elizabeth II made a point of travelling throughout the United Kingdom by revamped Royal Train for her Diamond Jubilee. This turned out to be a huge success with large crowds gathering to see her. There was also the added bonus of seeing a variety of locomotives at the front of the gleaming Royal carriages.

The imprimatur of Royal Train travel has over the decades been useful for the image of British Rail. Conversely, trains have been useful in boosting the image of the British monarchy. In the 19th century stream trains, the upstart new mode of transport, with their soot and noise were not always readily taken to by the people. However, with Queen Victoria setting a splendid example, often travelling in her luxuriously appointed Royal carriage, the chattering and wealthy classes quickly switched from horse and carriage to train travel.

The aristocracy of the period, who were of course almost always both chattering and wealthy, took a little longer to utilise the new phenomenon of the train. Michael Robbins details in his book *A Railway Age* a curious occurrence in the early days when aristocrats would depart their train as it neared London and meet up with their horse-drawn carriages for the final leg of the journey to their downtown residence. This was one way of avoiding the risk of the crime and grime of Paddington or Waterloo terminals. Another reason, advanced by Sam Burgess, former chairman of Australia's Zig Zag Railway, was that many of the aristocracy's town residences were located on the western side of central London. It was simply easier and quicker to avoid the big terminals and proceed home by one's own coach.

Almost overnight, mobility on a scale never before dreamt of became a reality. Journey times were slashed, so that a twelve hour journey was reduced to three hours, with a lot more comfort and safety attaching than provided by the horse. It was also possible for major events such as the Great Exhibition of 1851 to be organised as trains allowed many thousands, who otherwise would not have had the opportunity, to travel to London's Hyde Park to see the Crystal Palace.

On the main London–Manchester route the journey took 18 hours and 30 minutes by horse and coach in 1836. By rail, the journey time was slashed to just 5 hours in 1852, then 4 hours 15 minutes in 1887, 3 hours 30 minutes in 1914, 3 hours 15 minutes in 1939 and by 1985 a mere 2 hours 33 minutes.

British Virgin Rail has now introduced its new and very fast tilt train, the Pendolino, on this ever-growing route. On test runs in late 2002 the Pendolino made the trip in almost two hours. With further track improvements the trip takes two and a half hours, allowing for five stops. This is fully competitive with air, taking into account the saga of Heathrow Airport transfers. A trip on the separate and secondary Midlands route out of St Pancras to Manchester will still take around three hours. Over the decades, there has been spectacular progress in the United Kingdom in terms of train speed, although it will be much harder to cut another fifteen minutes off high-speed routes, such as the London to Manchester route, unless very high-speed TGV-type track and trains are introduced.

British Rail has designed its high-speed trains to have pull and push locomotives permanently at each end of train sets with five or more passenger carriages. This replaces the traditional concept of using one or two locomotives at the front to haul and having a guard's van and/or luggage van at the rear. What this has meant is much faster turn-arounds for passenger trains at the big terminals with their deadend platforms. Shunting locomotives from end to end costs money; it is far easier to have the driver walk from one end of the train to the other.

As Britain is the birthplace of the public railway, the best way for me to explain the modern British railway realm is with snapshots of some personal encounters. Let me begin with what I hoped would be a grand departure from Kings Cross station, London, the original terminus of the mighty London and North East Railway (LNER), post-Beeching. Despite a number of obvious moves to lower costs and boost efficiency, there were still some big gaps on all the remaining passenger operations.

As this visiting parliamentarian boarded the driver's cabin of a high-speed inter-city service to the north, he was greeted by the driver and his assistant, swearing about the 'chief dispatcher', who was nowhere to be seen. Barely two minutes before the appointed departure time, and with no more than a grunt, this official appeared and handed over the slip of paper with the running instructions for the 2.42 pm Kings Cross through York to Newcastle-upon-Tyne. The signal turned from red to green, the conductor gave the all clear, and we glided out of Kings Cross into the tunnel system to the north.

What did this chief dispatcher actually do, I asked. Could his job not have been done with an in-cabin fax? Could not the running instructions have been issued to the driver on signing on for his shift with updates by phone or radio phone? Could not the function have been eliminated? The answer was short, of course. It had always been done this way!

There are remnants of the best and worst of British Rail scattered right throughout the system. One noble and distinctive feature from the 19th century are the grand, curved platforms and stations such as Bristol Temple Meads of Great Western Railway fame and York in the Midlands on the LNER main line.

In recent years, these great stations have been upgraded to improve passenger usage, provide for more efficient freight yards and to cope with faster and faster trains. Express tracks which ran between the platform tracks have been removed at York and Bath, but the great curves, dictated by local geography and the use of short-length carriages, remain. This certainly enhances the vista of the station, but does nothing to improve the gaps created by the geometry between platform and the modern longer carriages.

Despite these problems, the grand curved platforms will remain. The cost to remove or straighten out the Bristol or York platforms would be prohibitive, not to mention unnecessary. York and Bristol are among the very best of Great Britain's restored stations.

Conversely, a revamp of Leeds City station in the 1960s was found wanting. This layout ensured congestion with nearly 1000 trains terminating, originating or passing through every day. The latest revamp in 2003 has taken the station to the cutting edge, with an increase in approach tracks and platforms. Best of all, was the success in combining the old and new to make the station a whole lot better for the 18 million people who pass through annually.

York is a wonderful place for the railway buff. Sitting just below the superb York Minster and the famous Shambles, a collection of very old buildings with irregular overhangs, some of which have in their basements the remnants of old Roman baths, is the magnificent National Railway Museum. On display in the museum are some of the iconic locomotives and carriages of yesteryear in mint condition, including Queen Victoria's original velvet and polished wood Royal carriage.

The York signal box boasted the largest and longest single frame of mechanical signal levers in the world with some 240 levers side by side stretching over 25 metres. In 1952 the signal box, which is long since gone, switched to an all electric panel system.

In 1988 during the parliamentary winter recess, I slipped away to visit India and then Britain to have a look at developments in transport infrastructure. Arriving in London on a Sunday in July to clear and sunny skies, I purchased a day return ticket to York.

At Doncaster I noticed a huge crowd of people hanging over the bridge linking the platforms. A large brass band had struck up nearby. Then suddenly it appeared in all its glory, the magnificent A4 Mallard steam engine, a superbly streamlined locomotive with sweeping lines and all decked out in rich, deep royal blue. This was a 50th anniversary of the Mallard's record breaking 126 miles per hour run recorded on 3 July 1938, the fastest time ever clocked by a steam locomotive anywhere in the world. The mint-condition Mallard was quickly hooked onto a set of luxury passenger carriages and readied for the re-enactment of that run across the Yorkshire Plains to York.

There is no doubt that the British railway realm excels at such ceremonial and sentimental re-enactments. This is the result of life-long commitment by many volunteers and Britain's good fortune in still having so much heritage rolling stock. Oh that it were thus elsewhere. In Australia the only four streamlined steam locomotives ever built for the Irish broad gauge system, including the famous Thomas Mitchell, were turned into scrap metal in the 1960s!

In Scotland and Wales there are many historical railways and tourist trains operating on a mix of standard and narrow gauges. Some run along spectacular coastlines just above sea level in narrow corridors between the beach and the mountains.

The best example of a coastline railway is the old Great Western Rail main line to Penzance, between Dawlish and Teignmouth, where the double track runs along a sea wall and through several tunnels. There is also a walking track for most of the section, allowing the opportunity to soak up the scenery, including a subtropical rainforest, and do some train spotting on this busy main line at the same time.

Fierce storms can cause waves to crash across the sea walls and tracks. This often results in salt spray entering sensitive wiring around the bogies causing shut-downs and leaving trains stranded in the surf, so to speak. Brunel would probably be cheered by the fact that the steam trains of his era would have made a better fist of these conditions than the superb, ultra modern but somewhat fragile, dainty and less than robust trains of today!

By a stroke of good luck, I was visiting this coastal section a couple of years ago to see the last regular service of Britain's first diesel locomotive, the Deltic. I asked a question of a companion as the train approached only to be roundly chastised by a train spotter videoing the event. 'Silence!' he screamed to all and sundry as he tried to capture the purity of the sound of the locomotive. Now, even I viewed this as being a bit over the top.

At the tail end of the 21st century, British Rail underwent a series of upheavals as a result of privatisation, including bankruptcies and system breakdowns. At much the same time there was a spate of tragic fatal crashes, which dominated the headlines for months.

Debate still rages about privatisation, both about the general benefits and the way the British government went about it. In the early 1990s, John Major's Conservative government continued the Margaret Thatcher agenda, setting up the privately owned Railtrack Corporation, which was basically responsible for track maintenance, and the Strategic Rail Authority, which was responsible for the issue of franchises to companies such as Virgin Rail to operate the networks. The Office of Rail Regulator, an independent body to regulate the whole system, was established as was a separate safety inspectorate.

In 1997 with the election of Tony Blair's Labour government, the ongoing agony of trying to graft new operators and owners on to the world's oldest system continued. A series of rail accidents between 1996 to 2003 pointed to the fact that the system was not being maintained and renewed as it should have been. Then, adding to the burden, Railtrack went financially belly up and the government had to step in to create Network Rail in mid 2002. In a form of partial nationalisation, Network Rail operates as a not-for-profit trust to run the rail infrastructure of Britain and plough profits back into maintenance and improvements.

Having said all this, privatised rail in Great Britain is really only six years old. According to Tom Windsor, the United Kingdom's Rail Regulator, the privatised system deserves time to prove itself. The truth is, however, that there is still a long way to go. The north–south system still has no high-speed main lines, the lack of double-stacked container trains limits freight opportunities and regional express capacity does not exist for the London underground and the other big cities. It will be both a bold and brave government that takes on these important challenges in the future. But unless they are dealt with, Britain's catch up and patch up mentality will ensure Europe and the other realms continue to dominate rail development.

There have, however, been some great successes in the last decade, the high point being the opening of the Euro Tunnel, from Folkestone to Calais. The London–Paris Eurostar is winning thousands back to train travel. The service will be further improved once a track between Folkestone and St Pancras station is completed, allowing the Eurostar to at last sweep towards London at high speed.

In September 2003 Prime Minister Tony Blair opened the first stage of this track, from Folkestone to Pepper Hill. It is the first new main line to be built in a greenfield in Great Britain since the 19th century. Construction of stage two from Pepper Hill to London, under the Thames, attracted an international workforce, including Sam Kelly, an engineer from Canberra, Australia. An unusual aspect of this job for Sam was the hazard of unexploded ordnances left over from the intense bombing of London's East End during World War II. 'Suddenly the yell would go up, something metallic had been struck by the excavator machinery. Everyone would quickly scatter until the bomb clearance people had checked it all out and destroyed the old bombs. Never have I seen so many machine drivers move so quickly,' Sam recalled.

Stage two traverses both above and below ground through the

north-east quarter of greater London, passing just north of Kings Cross station and then through a sweeping curve into an enlarged St Pancras terminal. It also allows for London to be bypassed, by high-speed trains from major British cities such as Leeds direct to Paris or Lyons.

Many 'nimbys', including former British Prime Minister Ted Heath, attempted to block this route for many years. However, its worth was quickly demonstrated when trial runs slashed the London to Paris journey to a record-breaking 2 hours 18 minutes, and the London to Brussels trip to just 1 hour 58 minutes. Regular runs in 2004 are timetabled at 2 hours 35 minutes and 2 hours 20 minutes respectively, a far cry from the old train/ferry/train trip across the English Channel.

Taking the gloss off this success, however, is the fact the Euro Tunnel after nearly a decade of safe operations is still in the red with annual losses exceeding US$2 billion. In 2003 freight movements were a mere 1.7 million tonnes, about one-quarter of the forecast levels, and total passenger movements were just over six million, well down from the ten million forecast.

To be fair freight was badly affected by sluggish European economies at the start of the 21st century and security shut-down the result of refugees stowing away on Euro Tunnel freight trains. Terrorist activities worldwide have also impacted on passenger numbers but with travel times having been further slashed in 2004, increased patronage is expected.

Despite the problems, elegant excellence can still be found in the United Kingdom. The Royal Scotsman operates out of Edinburgh in spring and summer, travelling across the Highlands allowing vistas of ancient castles and of primordial lochs. The five day trip offers all the best Scotland and British Rail of yesterday, right down to kippers and haddock for breakfast, not to mention the malt whisky of course.

I happily recall my first train trip in Scotland, travelling from Edinburgh to Aviemore in brilliant sunshine with my best man to be, Bill

Baxter, after a dump of snow the night before. We were sitting in the pleasant dining car enjoying table service, drinking Scotch whisky, eating Scotch soup and Scotch steak when Bill rescued my meal mid slide as we went around a sharp bend. I confess I was a nip or three ahead of him on the occasion!

This jaunt in 1975 was part of my first ever trip abroad, as a twenty-something bachelor and backbencher in the New South Wales state parliament. While I had been posted to Vietnam as an Army officer with the 1st Battalion in 1968 and 1969, and had gone to Singapore and Taiwan, I did not count these trips as travelling as they did not involve trains!

I learned a lot about trains on my first trip to the birthplace of rail, but most particularly that trains were a great deal faster than anything I had experienced in Australia. It was a revelation on the inter-city express back from Glasgow to Euston that trains offered some real competition to the airlines.

Against all odds, fast passenger trains have taken on air travel head to head and, at least on some routes such as Paris–Lyons and Paris–London, the stage has been set for intense competition.

Still, some things never change. I well recall the air becoming very frosty during a briefing session with senior British Rail officials in the 1970s when I remarked on the successful early progress of the Paris–Lyons TGV. One official sniffed that it was still to complete its first decade of operation, and in any case, a TGV had come off the rails when shunting. Millions of safe, fast passenger kilometres later, it has to be said the TGV has proved to be well ahead of anything on the British side of the English Channel.

As the major anniversaries of the creation of rail approach—the Oystermouth (the first horse-hauled passenger railway) in 2007, the Stockton–Darlington (first locomotive-hauled railway) in 2025, the Liverpool–Manchester Railway in 2030—it should always be remembered that all of these firsts occurred in the United Kingdom. So whatever else happens, no one can take the title away from Great Britain that it was the birthplace of the railway.

CHAPTER SEVEN

EUROPE: LEADING IN HIGH SPEED RAIL

If in Europe go by train, by very fast train of course. Do not pass Paris but do go straight to Le Train Bleu, the wonderful first floor restaurant at Gare de Lyon, one of Paris' three major train stations. This is the best advice I can offer to experience the most dynamic and magnificent modern railways, those of the heavily subsidised European realm.

Mind you, even in this most efficient of realms things can go wrong. I recall my absolute panic when left stranded at Portbou, the break of gauge between France and Spain. It was winter, before dawn and the wind was blowing hard, chilling me to the core. I had disembarked a train from Lyons, which had reached the end of the standard gauge, and went looking for the Spanish Imperial broad gauge train connecting to Valencia. Supposedly departing at 5.20 am, it simply did not eventuate that day.

In the gloom of early morning, and as if to tease me, a sparkling southbound high-speed Talgo overnight express swept in to the platform for a crew change and technical stop. No passengers were allowed on or off this unique train as its bogies slowly changed gauge width over a special section of track allowing a through service to operate on the French and Spanish networks.

I approached the Talgo conductor standing in the open doorway to ask if I could join his train. I can still remember his clear-cut 'No Mister' and associated burst of bad language. Somehow expletives are always recognisable no matter what language!

As the Talgo slid off into the dawn without me, I rechecked the display board in the half light to discover that while the next train to Valencia would leave at around 7.00 am, the one due at 8.00 am would actually get to Valencia one hour earlier. What a travel dilemma: to take the slow train you see waiting or wait for the fast train that might never turn up. I decided to not board the slow train and watched it depart, right on time with many spare seats. At one minute to eight the fast train had still not turned up. As this was in the wondrous days before mobile phones, I was starting to panic that I would not make my complex series of connections in Valencia. A very crowded fast train did turn up five minutes late and I offered a quiet cheer when it eventually passed the slow train to Valencia!

My personal travails on this occasion, however, were nothing compared to those of the Eurostar passengers travelling from London to Paris on 7 February 2003. Just a few kilometres out from Waterloo on a relatively new section of flyover, an air pipe fractured in new rolling stock. Passengers were kept on board for five hours as repeated attempts were made to haul the crippled train back to a platform. With no air circulating, those on board were becoming desperate, breaking windows to let much needed oxygen into the carriages. Some passengers tried to climb out of the windows, dangerously close to a live 1500-volt direct current for a nearby track. Rescue locomotives were available but they had the wrong couplings. It took many hours for the distressed passengers to be released.

The very best systems such as Eurostar are, after all, only as good as their weakest link. Speedy and safe recovery in breakdowns is absolutely important at all times. It has been thus since 1845 when the first steam trains started operations to and from Gare Du Nord in Paris.

There was one outstanding advantage conferred on the European railway realm from the very start and that was, with the exception of Portugal and Spain, Europe adopted the Stephenson standard gauge. This meant no costly breaks of gauge across borders, although there were some curious cross-over complications. France and Belgium, for example, run their trains, including TGVs, on the left-hand side of double-track main lines, whereas Germany and most other European countries run on the right-hand side. Trains heading west from Cologne to Brussels, for example, have to cross from the left side to the right side just near the border.

Still, the fact that there was no break of gauge was a great help in boosting rail in Europe, as were national treasuries ready to subsidise railway systems despite big losses being chalked up on both passenger and some freight services.

France and Italy sought to link their rail networks from an early date and commenced building a huge tunnel, the Cenis Tunnel, under the alps in 1857. As it would take a decade or more to complete the tunnel, the two governments also agreed to build a temporary track over Mount Cenis. This became the world's first railway linking two countries, at more than a mile above sea level.

With grades of 1 in 10, a unique system was applied to the project: the Fell centre rail system. This involved a set of steel wheels being locked on to a double-headed raised centre rail. A unique 3' 7½" (1105 mm) gauge was also chosen.

As recorded in *Railway Wonders of the World* by Frederick Talbot, this link from St Michel in France to Susa in Italy became the trail blazer for international mountain connections. Unfortunately, it operated for less than four years, although it did carry some 150 000 passengers in that time. The agreement between France and Italy was that once the deep Cenis Tunnel opened, the line over the mountain would be closed. Today, France and Italy are considering building a longer and deeper 50 kilometre tunnel.

The development of rail in France, like most of Europe, was affected by war and depression. Much of the railway network in northern France was destroyed during the Great War, and the Great Depression imposed its dead hand on development.

On 1 January 1938, the Societe Nationale des Chemins de fer Francais, or SNCF, was formed. This absorbed the main line companies such as the Paris, Lyons and Mediterranean railway and the Chemins de fer du Nord. (Fascinatingly, *Chemins de fer* is translated as 'the way of iron'.) With the SNCF, the vehicle had been created that was to spearhead rail development in France.

SNCF showed that high-speed train technology could be developed on standard gauge. The TGV Atlantique, which runs from Paris to Bordeaux, for many years held the world speed record of 515 kilometres per hour. However, more importantly, SNCF was able to achieve a reliability for its high-speed trains that dominates to this day.

All this French achievement has created a certain grand bearing, some might say arrogance, in the French. This I decided to tackle head on during a breakfast in Paris with the Australian ambassador to France at the time, John Spender, and the French minister for agriculture, Jean Glavany. Paris is a city of enormous beauty but at the time of my visit there existed a peculiar political dichotomy in this seat of French government: the president, Jacques Chirac, was right-wing and the prime minister, Lionel Jospin, was left-wing.

Jospin's minister was a kind, elderly former school teacher from south of Lyons, which happened to be one of the areas most heavily subsidised by the European Common Agricultural policy. As Australia's minister for trade, I naturally raised the issue of farm subsidies during our breakfast. The exchange of words I vividly recall, culminated with an admission by the minister for agriculture: 'You know something, Mr Fischer, the part of French agriculture that does the best is actually non-subsidised products, such as cut flowers, that fall outside the common agriculture policy.'

Of course, I seized on this and asked why France persisted with its hard line support for the policy. With a smile and a gesture to the sweeping view of Paris from the ambassador's window, the minister responded: 'It is the Parisians. They must have their view of tidy farms with hedges and a tapestry of crop colours to gaze at as they sweep past in the TGV.'

I immediately offered a simple solution. If France abolished the common agricultural policy, Australia would pay for clipsal screens to be fitted to each TGV window so videotapes could be run of pretty farmlands. Alas the breakfast ended soon after without the minister taking up the offer.

It is ironical that the mighty and at times haughty France stayed strongly committed to Stephenson standard. For years, France tried its own non-compatible Internet and even objected to the concept of Greenwich Mean Time (GMT) being established. For 27 years after the Greenwich meridian was adopted as the prime meridian for longitude, the French said, 'Non'. From 1884 to 1911, they insisted that 'Paris Mean Time', 9 minutes and 21 seconds behind GMT, be used![1]

GMT meant that local time zones could be rationalised. Eventually, with the arrival of long distance railways, national time zones were created based on GMT. Most European countries adopted one time zone covering the entire country. Even Russia attempted this, but with some confusion. All trains ran on Moscow time, timetables were printed to Moscow time and meals were served at Moscow time, even though the network operated across many time zones.

The railways of Europe continue along the path of high-speed technology. Spain swallowed hard and adopted a TGV-type standard gauge for its high-speed trains, despite the rest of its network being Iberian Imperial broad gauge.

Today European railways lead the way with high-speed train technology. The Europeans are also gradually applying more effort to rail freight after a long period of favouring freeways and tollways, and the

---

1. *Longitude: the true story of a lone genius who solved the greatest scientific problem of his time*, Dava Sobel, Fourth Estate, London, 1995

use of trucks. Having one standard gauge has helped, but there are some other factors at play.

First and foremost, is the economic 'wet' approach taken by many of the governments of continental Europe since World War II. Funds were poured into the public transport sector. Yes, freeway expansion was prolific, but rail funding and expansion was also taking place at a hectic pace. Not only in France with the development of the TGV system but in Germany with its ICE high-speed network and in Italy with the Pendolino high-speed tilt system, many sections of which are on elevated track. The generosity of treasuries in Europe when it came to investment in rail infrastructure has not really been replicated elsewhere. European governments appear to have an almost automatic acceptance that major rail upgrading projects are needed, despite the financial deficits.

Laced with this is the ever-present notion of national pride. If France could win the world rail speed record in the 1950s, then every effort had to be made by the other European countries to ensure they beat France.

The French SNCF has established some formidable speed records. In 1954, an all-electric locomotive reached a speed of 225 kph (140 mph), burying the 1939 Italian record of 203 kph (126 mph) made on a run between Florence and Milan just before World War II. In 1964 Japan introduced the Shinkansen but the French were not to be left behind. An early model TGV established a speed of 380 kph (236 mph) in 1981 and less than ten years later, the new TGV Atlantique put down that incredible and for many years unbeaten record 515 kph (320 mph).

The development of the European network was also helped by a loading gauge above rail that was much higher and wider than in Great Britain, thus greatly aiding the expansion of freight, especially full-size container carry-on rail. Known as Berne loading gauge, this generous gauge also allowed for double-decker commuter carriages to be used, for example on the Chantilly main line north-east of Paris.

Early rail engineers in Europe had more space and used it to advantage. Vertical height above top of rail in France is a generous 14' (4270 mm) versus a squat 11' 6" (3506 mm) in Great Britain. Track width in France is about 10' 4" (3150 mm) versus 8' 9" (2666 mm) in the Old Dart, so trains on the same standard gauge in France can be almost one-fifth higher and one-sixth wider than in Britain. Euro Tunnel operators are building an intermodal freight depot at Folkestone where the large European loading gauge now ends, to try and build on the 1.5 million tonnes of freight currently using the Channel Tunnel (Chunnel).

The Euro Tunnel has forced some European passenger train loading gauges to change. Eurostar train sets are narrower than those of the TGVs and fit snugly on both the British and European systems. The cost of expanding loading gauge, lifting bridges and enlarging tunnels in Britain would have been too high to justify.

For all the advantages offered by European rail networks, including having major terminals in city centres (one place airports can't be expanded or built) and the ability to increase capacity without taking precious space by using faster trains and improved signalling, problems remain. Fierce patriotism still exists, particularly in areas where the European Commission can be told to get lost. As a result, freight trains crew changes on borders remain a costly practice. Qualifying drivers for operation on adjoining systems requires considerable and expensive training.

Securing pathways for freight trains on busy passenger lines is another problem. Although not insurmountable, it is difficult if the computerised train control and signalling systems are not up to scratch, such as in the former eastern bloc countries.

Germany and France are big users of rail freight, but as figures for 2000–01 show freight tonnage in Germany was down 2.3 per cent, France 9 per cent and Greece 11 per cent. Conversely, Great Britain was up 8.8 per cent and Ireland up 5.3 per cent. The great competitor, modern road freight hammering down the autobahns and tollways, continues to grow each year.

A mixture of the old, low standard, slow tracks of eastern Europe with the new, high standard tracks of western Europe has caused slow running services, bottlenecks and under-performance of high-powered locomotives. This was brought home to me when travelling from Hamburg to Berlin by DeutscheBahn before the Berlin Wall came down.

I had embarked from the mighty Hamburg Hauptbahnhoff, with its huge arch roof, right on time. We headed towards East Germany at a reasonable speed until we reached the border. There we stopped and were put through a very strict customs and security inspection. Crossing into East Germany was like entering a time warp. Farmers still used horses to pull their ploughs, just a few roads were sealed and the train track was made of very short lengths of rail, had unwelded joints and little ballast. We travelled at a tortuously slow speed until we reached the edge of West Berlin, and crossed back onto modern tracks, zipping into Berlin's famous Zoologischer Garten station.

I flew out of Berlin, on this my first visit to the city. The first leg of the flight was rather eerie until I worked out that the jet was flying at propeller height. It seems the Russians had imposed a restriction stipulating a maximum flying height over East Germany of 10 000 feet. As a result, on this clear afternoon there was much to see, including an aerial view of a very run down transport infrastructure. Today great progress has been made on this and the other corridors that once linked Germany to the then isolated city of West Berlin.

Mark Pierce, partner of Australia's ambassador to the European Union, Joanna Hewitt, tells a very different story of his experience on a DeutscheBahn train from Berlin. Having decided to do some Christmas shopping at Cologne's famous Christmas market he realised his onward ticket to Brussels and his travel pass had been pickpocketed. Standing on the platform at Cologne station, he made a split-second decision and jumped onto the previously booked international express, the Thalys. He hoped he could sweet-talk his way across the German–Belgian border to Brussels.

Finding the conductor in the very last car, Mark began to explain his predicament in halting German. The conductor smiled and asked if he was Mark Pierce. Absolutely stunned, Mark replied, 'Yes'. A known pickpocket had been arrested on the crowded concourse a few minutes before the train left and Mark's pass and ticket were found on him. Station police handed Mark's missing documents to the conductor, who then offered him a quiet place to sit and a cool drink.

Mark wrote to the head of DeutscheBahn to express his thanks. Miracles, however, do have their limits. Mark never received a reply to his letter.

Clearly, there can be no complacency even in Europe, as it surges ahead with innovation and expansion of its railways. Spectacular new connections such as the Channel link between France and Great Britain and the magnificent Oresund Bridge from Denmark to Sweden can only suggest a positive future. Despite some cooling of economic growth and the resultant clipping of rail subsidies by European treasuries, there is little doubt that the 21st century will be good for rail in the European realm. Long periods of high fuel prices will further boost rail's growth in the coming decades.

CHAPTER EIGHT

NORTH AMERICA:
A BITTERSWEET VIEW OF RAIL

North America did not lead the world with the inception of the railway, but the United States, in particular, quickly caught on to the idea of rail freight, leading its development for over two centuries. Five names jump out as being the godfathers of rail freight in the United States: Sam Golden, who developed intermodal out of Chicago in the 1930s; Gene Ryan, who pushed container and piggyback engineering in the 1950s; Malcolm McLean, who developed the new generation road/rail/ship containers; David DeBoer, who was both a regulator briefly and a railroader; and Mike Mohan of Southern Pacific Railways, who developed the idea of double-stacking.

Freight trains were essential in opening up the country and played an important part in the stories of the Wild West. In 1975, the cruel but necessary step was taken to start eliminating the caboose, or guard's van, from the rear of freight trains, bittersweet progress ending decades of rail history and colourful folklore. While freight train crews were reduced by one-third overnight, shunting and overall productivity was greatly boosted. Safety concerns were resolved with a simple device that included a flashing light attached to the last freight wagon.

Almost inevitably, it was in a Holiday Inn coffee shop in Bloomington, Illinois in early 1975 that the fateful meeting took place when it was agreed to 'take out' the caboose.[1]

An ugly cloud hung over the meeting and that was the very real threat of bankruptcy, railroad closure and massive job losses if a new approach was not adopted. The union leaders present had the very difficult task of justifying this change to their members. It was agreed that a trial on the Chicago–St Louis corridor would take place and that two-man crews and a slingshot approach to rosters would be adopted, eliminating the need for overnight crew stays.

This approach became an industry benchmark. Thousands of guard's vans were eliminated around the world and workforces were slashed, but rail freight productivity was boosted in the nick of time, offering fierce competition to aggressive road freight operators.

American freight rail had developed its own culture. The train guard, or conductor, shared the caboose with the rear brakeman and, for some trains, a flagman. The forward and rear brakemen became part of American folklore, having to work in all sorts of conditions, from snow and ice through to searing desert heat. They were rugged individuals, danger men, who often lost fingers and had bones crushed on the job as they coupled and de-coupled wagons. Even with nicknames such as 'Pinhead' and 'Shack Stinger', sadly, they weren't rugged enough to survive the introduction of modern communication, or the abolition of the caboose.

I discovered rail in the United States by accident. I had run out of money in San Francisco during my first trip to the United States and Mexico in 1971. This was in the days before I owned a credit card and I had to fill the ten hour wait for my flight back home in some way. Instead of sitting on a park bench, I decided to walk the city of San Francisco and part of Oakland looking at the fantastic cable cars

---

1 As detailed by David DeBoer (for a brief period a railway regulator and for many years a railway marketing and operational manager) in his book, *Piggyback and Containers*.

and as much of the rail system as I could see without having to spend a cent.

In a lucky break, I spied a front page notice in the local newspaper that the mayor of San Francisco would be sworn in at 11.00 am and there would be free doughnuts and coffee. I walked to the town hall and dutifully attended the swearing-in of a mayor who, a couple of years later, was sent to jail on corruption charges. I confess to having eaten some twenty doughnuts. I needed all the sustenance I could get to see me through my day of transport inspections and my flight out of town. Needless to say, I have not voluntarily eaten a doughnut since.

While I could not afford to ride on San Francisco's extraordinary cable cars that day, I did watch them operate on the city's steep hills. Their cable grips had them jerking and jolting and flying around the corners of this bustling city, one of the five most distinctive and beautiful big cities of the United States. The others, in my humble view, are Boston, Washington, New Orleans and, of course, New York. Sadly, only San Francisco has cable cars, but the other cities do score well with conventional railways and even suburban commuter rail.

The 'pièce de résistance' of urban rail in the United States is the San Francisco Bay Area Rapid Transit System (BART), which was being built during my moneyless visit to the city. Opened in 1972, this Rolls Royce subway and surface system is bettered by few systems anywhere in the world, except perhaps Singapore. In 1962, a famous referendum or proposition ballot was held in San Francisco. Voters were asked to support the BART and the necessary huge bond finance program to build it. The proposition gained an overwhelming 60 per cent 'yes' vote.

Ten years later, on 11 September 1972, BART commenced operations. It faced some teething problems, including derailments and overshoots through buffers. According to Stan Fischler in *Subways of the World* BART proved its worth at 5.04 pm on 17 October 1989, when the Loma Prieta earthquake hit California. Its heavy duty rails and the curious use of 5' 6" Imperial broad gauge helped BART survive relatively undamaged allowing it to operate the following day. Usage jumped from 219 000 to 357 000 passengers daily. At last, the cynics and the freeway fanatics of California had to eat humble pie.

San Francisco today has a diverse public transport system, envied by many around the world. It is a far cry from the very unwise era between World Wars I and II when rail track was ripped up all over the country, often by syndicates operating bus networks with links to Detroit, the car manufacturing capital of the United States. Indeed, the suburban electric systems in San Francisco and a number of other cities were completely shut down during this period.

Railways came to North America at about the same time as Europe. Like many other realms, different main line gauges operated, particularly in the east-ern half of the United States. Thankfully these were all switched to standard gauge by 1890. Where North America differed from the European realm, for example, was that it was big enough to support many transcontinentals, the very first coming together at Promontory, Utah. At 12.47 pm on 10 May 1869, a famous Western Union telegram was dispatched across the United States with the simple word 'Done', announcing that the track from the east had joined the track from the west. Many preparations had been made to ensure the telegram was dispatched just as the last spike was being driven in. Telegraph lines were kept clear across the Union to ensure the exciting news reached both coasts as quickly as possible.

Canada's first transcontinental took a little longer to build, with construction commencing in 1875. The many engineering challenges encountered, especially over the Rockies, slowed construction so it was not until 7 November 1885 that the Montreal to Vancouver link was completed.

The history of the Canadian transcontinental was not unlike the east–west transcontinental in Australia. The colony of British Columbia on the west coast of Canada, just like the colony of Western Australia, demanded an east–west railway as a condition for entry into Federation.

Of course, Canada eventually went one better than Australia and ended up with not one but three transcontinental routes through the Rockies (over Yellowhead Pass at 3717 feet, Kicking Horse Pass at 5326 feet and Crowsnest Pass at 4459 feet). For many years Canadian National Railways, which was formally established in 1923, operated a service from Winnipeg to the west coast to compete with the Canadian Pacific, which led the way into Vancouver.

The story of the railways of the North America is dominated by the fact that over the decades this realm has handled the development of rail freight brilliantly, but has maintained a love/hate relationship when it comes to passenger services. The struggle continues to this day, although an occasional effort has been made to turn this around. Los Angeles, for example, is slowly building a modern metro system, which in 2003 saw the opening of the new Gold Line from Pasadena to downtown Los Angeles.

In an attempt to prevent the elimination of passenger trains in Canada and the United States altogether, rail operators on both sides of the border have looked at consolidating services. In Canada all rail passenger services, excluding commuter, were switched to a new entity called VIA. Since 1977 VIA has cut back services on many branch lines but has also continued to develop smarter trains, with heavy emphasis on passenger comfort and service. (It is said that the first railway dining car was introduced in Canada in 1867.) From my own limited experience of travelling on VIA trains around Montreal and Toronto, the needs of the passenger are obviously important, with extra baggage assistance and plenty of information provided.

This is in sharp contrast to Amtrack, which was set up in the United States at around the same time as VIA to handle long-distance passenger train services. For many years stories would regularly emerge from the United States claiming that Amtrack was about to close, that Congress had not agreed to provide any more funding and that the all-powerful road lobby had ensured its funding almost to the exclusion of rail. From its inception Amtrack has carried less than 1 in every 100 inter-city travellers in the United States, the other 99 preferring to go by air, coach and car. However, in 1999 Amtrack enjoyed a record year of passenger travel. The service from Boston to Washington via New York has been further improved with the introduction of the Acela Express, which zips along at 150 miles per hour. While it is well utilised and competitive, the Acela is still much slower than regular TGV services in France.

There is no doubt the freeways of the United States, from the super turnpikes of New York to the very western end of Route 66 in downtown Los Angeles, lead the world in terms of road engineering. It is also true that air travel remains extremely popular and relatively cheap in the United States, despite 9/11 and the ongoing threat of terrorism. The squeeze that motor vehicle and air travel have put on rail services means that Amtrack struggles from year to year.

All of this is a bit curious, given that a number of the main lines in the United States travel along some truly spectacular routes, such as the coastal route from Los Angeles to San Francisco and the water route from New York to Chicago along the edge of Lake Erie.

One of the less well-known but truly spectacular trips is from New York to Montreal along the Hudson River and past Lake Champlaine. I first travelled on the daily Amtrack-operated 'Adirondack' one sunny, early autumn day in 1980. Departure was from New York Grand Central Station, deep below the magnificent main hall of this superb station. (Today the Adirondack has been relegated to the crowded and far from grand Penn Station.) I waited in the main hall until the departure and arrivals board flashed the signal that the doors to the platform had been opened. (In the curious way that distinguishes railway cultures around the world, passengers at Grand Central must wait in the main hall and aren't allowed on the platforms until just before departure.) I made my way quickly to my reserved seat and awaited departure, which on this day was right on time. Soon we were heading north out of New York and along the Hudson River Valley with its steep banking cliffs on either side.

I spotted the famous West Point Military Academy but could not find Hyde Park, the huge home and museum of President Franklin

Delano Roosevelt, the only president ever to be elected four consecutive times to the White House, in 1932, 1936, 1940 and 1944. I vowed to return one day with my family to see this important museum. As president, FDR often travelled by train from Washington to Warm Springs near Atlanta, Georgia, where he maintained a small version of the White House known as the 'little White House'. This is where he died in 1945, shortly after the Yalta Conference with Stalin and Churchill.

I calculated that Roosevelt had travelled by train more than any other president of the United States, partly because he was in the position longer, but also because trains made it easier for him to get around in his wheelchair. Today it is rare for a president to travel by train, although Bill Clinton made a point of travelling from Washington to Chicago by train when his nomination as Democrat candidate for the presidency was confirmed in 1996.

We arrived at Albany, the capital of New York State, a place from which many national political careers have been launched, including Nelson Rockefeller for the Republicans and Franklin Delano Roosevelt for the Democrats. The Adirondack was pleasant to travel in with its open-style carriages and reasonably good catering. However, my enduring memory of this stop-over concerned something a whole lot more earthy. I all too vividly recall a sewage pump-out truck coming alongside while the train was at the platform and proceeding about its business carriage by carriage. Unfortunately, at our carriage, the pump-out pipe became dislodged and a truly horrendous stench enveloped the train. It was with us for 30 minutes, until we eventually resumed our northbound journey.

One of the hazards of operating long-distance passenger trains on a shoestring is the need to carry out maintenance on the run. It was cheaper to service the train in Albany than either New York or Montreal. My unfortunate experience was certainly something you wouldn't expect to happen on one of the best trains in the United States or Canada, and one of the few truly international services in North America.

The really good news in North America concerns freight. There is a great deal of intermodal road to rail traffic, as well as ship to rail traffic, particularly at Los Angeles. Huge double-stacked container freight trains now move quickly, and profitably, between the port of Los Angeles and Chicago and other important junctions and hubs, including New York. The only problem is congestion at port as a result of huge container pile-ups.

In 1977, the Southern Pacific Railroad, headquartered at Los Angeles, led the United States and the world in developing double-stacked container operations. Southern Pacific in concert with the ocean shipper Sealand and the auto builder ACF developed wagons that had end bulkheads and two separate bogies.

In 1982, a second generation wagon, or more accurately set of wagons, was developed by American President Lines in liaison with Thrall Car Manufacturing. These had no heavy end bulkheads. Container couplings had improved so much that the wagons could be articulated into groups of five, with the bogies being shared between each wagon. As a result, the number of dual-axle bogies was reduced by four, and heavy couplings were reduced by eight, allowing containers to be moved a lot more quickly and efficiently.

Mike Mohan, who was previously with Southern Pacific but is now based in Perth with ARG, believes that double-stacking saved the day for the rail freight business during a critical period when many railroads were going bust. Thanks to the early work of Southern Pacific, 20 per cent of railroad freight in the United States today goes by double-stacked container.

Freight rail in both Canada and the United States has been very profitable over the years and remains so today. The percentage of freight going by rail is much higher in the United States than Europe, while the passenger ratio is the other way around.

Sadly, Mexico cannot claim the same success as the United States or Canada even though it uses the same standard gauge system.

The British helped put down the first railway line in Mexico from the port of Vera Cruz to Mexico City. With its sharp climb up from the coast and some challenging terrain, this line, which took some 28 years to build, was completed in 1873. In more recent decades, the French helped install a magnificent but very crowded subway system in Mexico City. Every tunnel built unearthed more and more magnificent Aztec artifacts. Important archaeological finds either had to be bypassed or carefully extracted and preserved to be showcased in the underground stations or at the magnificent Mexico Anthropological Museum.

Since 1950 there has been a steady decline in the operations of the Mexican railways. Almost all passenger services have been stopped, apart from the famous Copper Canyon train which travels through spectacular scenery in central Mexico. Trains no longer run along the famous great southern route from Mexico City to Cuernavaca. This spectacular standard gauge climbed steadily out of Mexico City, peaking on the rim of an old volcano before descending through two long lateral sweeps into the bustling and beautiful town of Cuernavaca. There are one or two successful tourist trains but the main railway station in Mexico City is virtually deserted.

Time will tell if the passenger railways of Mexico will bounce back. A huge investment will be required but given the success of the North American Free Trade Agreement, this certainly cannot be ruled out.

Following privatisation in 1995, several freight operators with links to American railroads have entered the field. The result has been significant expenditure and network upgrading of the routes down from the border with the United States. The largest operator, Transportacion Ferroviaria Mexicana has begun hauling automotive products, in particular, through the major border crossings with the United States.

There are a number of narrow gauge systems in Central America. The most important railway in the region, by far is the Panama Transcontinental, the world's first transcontinental railway. Built originally in 5' or Czar broad gauge, the whole operation was revamped in the 1990s and switched to standard gauge by the United States owners and operators, Norfolk and Southern. Double-stacked container freight trains bustle along this line from the Pacific Ocean to the Atlantic Ocean, a total distance of 80 kilometres. There are even daily passenger services. This railway line, built before the Panama Canal, continues to compete with shipping traffic, even with the great improvements to the canal over the decades.

One day I hope to undertake a journey through the Panama Canal, going by ship one way and back by train the other way. When I do this, I will be reminded of the fact that the axis of this transcontinental waterway and railway is neither east–west nor north–south. The axis is, in fact, north-west to south-east, reflecting the bend in the land bridge between North America and South America. This bit of trivia allows the declaration to be made that North America does not have a north–south transcontinental. Only Australia has a seamless north–south transcontinental without break of gauge!

The commitment to rail and the future of rail in North America is very mixed, notwithstanding some tremendous engineering feats, such as the laying of rail through the Rockies and the construction of the railway line from Miami to Key West. Just 250 kilometres long, it crossed 28 islands, as well as sea and marshes. It was literally built over seas. Opened in 1912, the railway was reasonably successful until a hurricane hit on Labor Day, 2 September 1935. With a barometer reading of 26.35 inches (892 hectopascals), the lowest ever recorded on land at the time, the hurricane smashed the railway to pieces, destroying bridge after bridge, viaduct after viaduct, and a rescue train as well. Several hundred people were killed and little was left standing in the huge storm and the huge tidal wave that surged a short time later. The Miami–Key West line was destined for an early death. Nature had comprehensively done over the engineers.

The railways of North America were more generally done over by another dynamic, a deeply embedded bias towards the motor vehicle and freeways. It is curious and frustrating that the realm that gave the world so many of the finest and most glamorous trains of last century—the Twentieth Century Limited from New York to Chicago, the Californian Zephyr from Chicago to San Francisco, the Aurora Express in Alaska—has at best a lukewarm regard for the role of the railway in the 21st century.

Growing congestion around the big cities of the United States will help force a rethink of priorities for rail. With greater utilisation of both passenger and freight services, will there be enough capacity to cope? In the land of the free, the answer is only a maybe.

CHAPTER NINE
SOUTH AMERICA DERAILS

It has to be said that the Incas, with their speedy runners, would have been able to send messages faster than the disconnected, dysfunctional, multi-gauge railways of South America. Sadly, the railways of South America have never realised their full potential, despite flashes of brilliance in the early days, and some of the grandest railway stations ever built anywhere in the world.

The mighty Retiro complex of stations, including the Belgrano station which dominates downtown Buenos Aires, was the setting off point for the dominant Imperial broad gauge system of Argentina. In the 1880s, you could depart on the Rosario Express at 12.25 pm from Belgrano station and after maintaining an average speed of well over 40 kilometres per hour arrive in Rosario at 7.38 pm, a distance of some 305 kilometres. Despite these impressive beginnings, which included relatively fast services from Buenos Aires to La Plata offered by two different companies on two different tracks, the Argentinian railway system is stagnant today.

If ever there was a corridor tailor-made for freight and fast international passenger service, then surely it should have been from Valparaiso in Chile to La Plata in Argentina via Santiago, a tunnel under the Andes to Mendoza and Buenos Aires. For this visionary route to have been built, Argentina and Chile would have had to have co-operated, a very unlikely proposition given the history of the two countries. Certainly, some brilliant engineering would have been required to build a tunnel under the Andes. (Charles Eiffel did travel to Chile and helped design part of the railway system, including Santiago's central station with its magnificent iron lattice work very similar to that which dominates the Eiffel Tower.) That tunnel through the Andes would have won freight to rail, particularly freight moving from the Pacific Ocean to the Atlantic, as it would have offered a way of avoiding the dangerous Straits of Magellan and Cape Horn. If such a corridor existed today, then a high-speed passenger service might be operating between the two great capital cities of South America, Buenos Aires and Santiago.

All of this is wishful thinking, of course, even though there is so much untapped potential in South America that building this corridor by degrees cannot be ruled out. Unfortunately, this will not happen before the centenary of the opening of the first rail link between Chile and Argentina in 2014. On the original Santiago to Mendoza link, there was a break of gauge on the mountain section where the rail became metre gauge with a rack and pinion operation. It was extraordinary that steam locomotives of the period could travel up the very steep one in eight grade slope.

In support of the dream corridor between Santiago and Buenos Aires, is the fact that the dominant gauge on both sides of the Andes is the same, namely Imperial broad gauge (5' 6" or 1676 mm). There are generally two reasons given why this wide gauge was chosen in much of South America. The first is because of the colonial connections that existed between many South American countries and Spain; the second is that British equipment and locomotives originally intended for India were diverted to Argentina. Trevor Rowe, in his excellent book on the railways of South America, explains that not only did Argentina receive the surplus British-built equipment destined for India, but that significant British investment in Argentina would have encouraged the Argentinian government in its choice of Imperial broad gauge.

Despite Imperial broad gauge being dominant in Argentina, there were disastrous breaks of gauge that mirrored what happened in Australia. No less than four main gauges were adopted. A small section of the network from Buenos Aires to the west was built in Stephenson standard gauge, much of the mountain track and some of the main lines back into the capital were built in metre gauge, while the old Patagonia Express ended up on track slightly smaller than the Suez Walhalla Whitfield gauge (of 762 mm or 2' 6"). Buenos Aires and Adelaide are the only two capital cities in the world that can boast operations using three main gauges.

I do confess, however, that in the case of Adelaide the claim is a little dubious as I have to rely on the Semaphore to Fort Glanville Railway, a tourist operation that runs along a beautiful beach corridor and that uses Semaphore narrow (457 mm or 1' 6"). This fort was built in the 19th century in response to a threat from the Russians. Neither the Russians nor their Czar broad gauge ever made it to the southern hemisphere. Anglo Cape narrow gauge is also laid out in Adelaide's enticing Port Dock National Railway Museum of Australia, the world's largest multi-gauge railway museum.

It was a very hot Sunday afternoon when I boarded a standard gauge steam train west of Buenos Aires for the run into the capital. I had just had a long and splendid lunch with the governor of Buenos Aires Province, a likely future president although not one of the five who revolved through the Pink Palace during 2002, a year of turmoil in Argentinian politics.

As we steamed along, it was clear we were travelling on a railway system that had fallen on very hard times. The telltale signs were all there: railway sleepers in need of replacement and old-style signalling. There were compensations, however, in the big smiles and helping hands offered by the friendly Argentinians who faced the challenge of operating the run-down system with good humour.

It is very likely that I annoyed my entourage with a barrage of questions about the history of rail in Argentina. The wiser diplomatic officials who travelled with me knew that I would always end up asking questions about local transport instead of studying the detailed briefing notes they supplied for the next day of meetings, interviews and speeches. Most were cunning enough to steer me back to my official chores and most managed to keep their cool despite my excessive demands that they get up early to join me in seeing some local life before the day's program began. Occasionally, I encountered an ambassador or deputy secretary who had the same interests as me!

I eventually learnt that my obsession with rail was tolerated by the Department of Foreign Affairs and Trade because it rounded out my knowledge of the country I was visiting, giving me a useful negotiating tool. It was also infinitely preferable to having to look after visiting members of parliament or their spouses who were more interested in shopping than anything else. Fortunately, my wife Judy hates shopping; she would rather visit an interesting aid or trade project, and journey to a refugee camp any day.

From Buenos Aires it was yet another midnight departure and early morning arrival in Colombia and then Santiago for more trade talks and the opening of the Australian Gas Light (AGL) Company's Chile office. Great economic progress has been made in Chile over the last 25 years, although there has been little commitment to or investment in the railway system apart from a new and greatly improved, all-electric service introduced from Santiago to Temuco in 2003.

The north–south axis of Chile lends itself to the development of one main trunk line, but there remains that all too common problem of a break of gauge. Imperial broad gauge dominates the southern half of Chile while metre gauge dominates the northern half, and is used to transport minerals and concentrates from the Atacama Desert to the port of Antofagasta. It was in the bare Atacama Desert and the incredible Valley of the Moon that I saw a moonscape on earth.

About 100 years ago, a number of mining and railway companies combined with the governments of Chile and Argentina to commence building the Northern Transadine Line between Antafagasta and Salta. It has operated on and off ever since, but was not completed until after World War II. For a period, a passenger and international sleeping car service ran on this line, taking four days to make it all the way from Antofagasta on the Pacific Ocean to Buenos Aires via Socompa.

When the line was built, the next to zero rainfall meant that little ballast was required. As a result, a long section of track above 10 000 feet could be laid directly on the earth. Had the construction engineers dug down a couple of metres, they would have uncovered the world's largest copper deposit at Escondida. The mine that was eventually established, and for many years owned and operated by BHP Australia, can be found along the track due east of Antofagasta in a spectacularly barren landscape several thousand feet above sea level. Perhaps too much wine was drunk along this line, making people blind to the world's largest copper find.

The mighty Andes have been conquered by rail in a couple of places, including between Chile and Bolivia, providing the shortest link from land-locked Bolivia to a sea port. Bolivian railways have seen better days. The main station at La Paz looks particularly lonely, but the railway is vital for Bolivian exports.

My brother Tony was travelling on a Bolivian train along this corridor in 1967, when news came through that the Australian prime minister, Harold Holt, had drowned off Cheviot Beach south of Melbourne. The Bolivian train crew were overcome with disbelief and deep concern. How could a country let its prime minister swim in dangerous waters? He could be eaten by a shark. And where were the life boats? The sympathy they extended to Tony was laced with much local wine.

Nearby Peru has the highest railway in the world, from Lima to Huancayo. Still operational, work on this railway commenced in 1870. Laid out in Stephenson standard gauge, many zig zags and tunnels were installed to help trains gain height as they climbed the Andes. The rail summit is just over 4800 m, so oxygen is provided for passengers. I have never travelled on this line, but I hope to do so one day with my family and with oxygen on hand.

The other famous South American railway on my must visit list is from Cuzco to Machu Picchu, the fabulous lost city in the clouds. The challenge of this railway is how to keep operating safely in such a high altitude. The heavy rainfall in the region causes hazardous land slips. In early 2004 this line was closed for many days when large sections of track were destroyed by such a landslide. Thankfully, no trains were toppled.

South America's biggest rail system is in Brazil. Again, a bizarre set of decisions were made ensuring break of gauge just about everywhere. In 1852 work commenced on a metre gauge system, known as the Leopoldina system, near Rio de Janeiro. But lest it feel lonely, Brazil also developed an Irish broad gauge system. Today about one-quarter of the network is broad gauge and the balance mainly narrow gauge. For a period, several other mountain gauges were also used.

Brazil also developed a unique cable grip rail system for the steep plunge from São Paulo to its port at Santos. Using steam engine-operated winching stations and a counter-balancing system, the trains going up the line balanced the weight of the trains coming down the line. It must have been an extraordinary sight in its heyday in the early part of last century, albeit slow to operate as trains had to be broken into small sections.

Unfortunately, like so many other countries in South America, in modern Brazil railways have fallen on very hard times. For many years a lack of investment meant that rail couldn't compete against the road trucking and powerful coastal and river shipping industries. Today there is a small resurgence with new track being built for freight use.

South America can claim two other distinctions. The first is the development of the unique Americas gauge (exactly 3' or 914 mm) used extensively in Colombia. The second is the Falklands Islands railway, the smallest in South America. Built during World War I at Port Stanley for defence communication requirements, the Cane narrow gauge of 2' or 610 mm was chosen for the section from the port to the large radio transmitter station some five kilometres to the west. It operated for several years conveying coal to the boilers to boost the signal from the transmitter stations. Seventy years later, during the Falklands War, Britain no longer needed that railway. Modern communication equipment made that transmitter station and its boilers long obsolete.

The Falkland Railway was unique in another way. Trevor Rowe details an extraordinary method of providing power to the tiny railway. On this island dominated by fierce westerly winds, a sail was used to power the train carriages on the easterly run home.

A lack of economic progress for long periods in the 20th century has resulted in large sections of South America's existing networks being lost forever. Many private railway companies failed, so most railways are now state-owned, although they are not seen as a priority for new capital investment.

As South America seeks to energise the Americas Free Trade Agreement, focus will eventually return to the development of transport infrastructure. It is vital that the railway be considered as part of that equation. As South America has some of the most polluted cities in the world, there is also a need to further develop commuter rail to deal with its serious environmental problems.

The railways of South America will need a lot more than wind power before they return to the glory days of a century ago when local economies boomed on beef and gold. In due course, I am confident that South America will again become economically successful and join the great rail recovery of the 21st century.

CHAPTER TEN

AFRICA: AGONY AND LUNACY

Cecil Rhodes had a grand vision for the African continent, a Cape to Cairo railway. Departing from Cape Town in South Africa and running through to Cairo in Egypt, it was to be a very long haul over huge mountain ranges, across high plateaus and ultimately down the Nile Valley to the delta and into Cairo and the port of Alexandria on the Mediterranean.

Sadly many wars, including the brutal Boer War, the various Sudan wars, and indirectly World Wars I and II intervened to prevent the project from going ahead. Rich in rivers and minerals, there has simply been too much agony, the burden of frequent famines, waves of epidemics and political corruption for the continent's great potential to be realised.

Rhodes' vision started well enough, at least when it came to gauge, with Egypt adopting standard gauge for the opening of the railway line from Alexandria to Cairo in 1856. A little later, this line was extended to the Gulf of Suez with access to the Red Sea. Robert Stephenson, the very busy son of George Stephenson, was the engineer-in-chief of the Egyptian Railways, thus ensuring that not only was standard gauge used, but that a good deal of the equipment required to operate railways in Egypt's harsh conditions was compatible.

Almost 150 years after its inception, I had the privilege of travelling by train from Cairo to Alexandria during a busy ministerial visit.
A smart looking turbo-powered, self-propelled train set of Spanish
design waited at the platform at Cairo railway station. Like so many
main stations in Africa and the Middle East, Cairo was seething with
people and burdened with baggage. There was also a good deal of
security, with armed soldiers in large numbers guarding the departure
platforms and station buildings. Well before September 11, Egypt
took the threat of terrorism very seriously. In 1981 the Egyptian president, Anwar Sadat, was assassinated during a military parade. Then, in
1997 over sixty tourists were killed in a terrorist attack at Luxor.
Despite the high-profile of so many soldiers all ready to shoot, their
presence was reassuring.

Once on board the Intercity Turbo, I was able to read up on the
briefing notes for the next round of meetings and keep abreast of the
cables and newspaper clippings forwarded on from Canberra through
the Australian Embassy in Cairo. It proved to be a very efficient way
to travel the relatively short distance between these two great cities.
On this particular day the train was clean, the ride was smooth, and
we arrived punctually in downtown Alexandria.

While the Egyptian railways, like so many railways of the world, is
in need of considerable investment and upgrading, a major modernisation project is taking place with the introduction of French
high-speed trains from Alexandria to Cairo. These will offer a one-
hour service from 2004, to be eventually extended further up the
Nile. Along with Great Britain and India, Egypt was one of the first
countries to introduce passenger rail services in the 19th century. It
is again at the forefront, and decades ahead of Australia, by being one
of the first countries outside Europe and Japan to introduce high-
speed train operations.

Immediately after arriving at Alexandria Station, I had to dash to
the port to see Australian bulk wheat being unloaded for delivery to
a large local flour mill. At one stage the mill's general manager took
me to one side as if to let me in on a great secret. I vividly recall

standing on the edge of the wharf as he told me how good Australian wheat was and how it was always delivered on time and within one or two per cent of specifications. He then pointed north and whispered he could never trust some of the other suppliers whose shipments were often contaminated with dust and weeds!

All of this was, of course, music to my ears as Australia's minister for trade. However, I was less than impressed when the general manager later told me that most of the flour from the mill in Alexandria was transported by road and not rail. This was an internal matter for Egypt so, of course, I made no comment but I did emphasise that Australia would always supply high quality wheat and thanked him for the business.

It was then a quick trip along the coast by car to El Alamein to visit the war graves and to see where the great desert battles of World War II took place. Instead of railway activity along the way, what we saw were huge beach resorts. Today, the line along the coast to the Libyan border is being upgraded, to link further west at Algeria to create a Trans North Africa route. As luck would have it, most of the railways in that direction are of standard gauge.

As I departed Egypt, I thought Cecil Rhodes had it right with his concept of a Cape to Cairo railway. Certainly Egypt would have made a great stepping off point for the long haul south. However, while Egypt remains locked into standard gauge, South Africa operates on Anglo Cape narrow gauge. Again, break of gauge stymied what could have been one of the great transcontinental railways of the world.

In his book *Atlas of the World's Railways* Brian Hollingsworth details how a standard gauge line was built out of both Durban and Cape Town to the hinterland in 1860. Climbing out of the coastal plains, both lines came to an early halt when the British government intervened from London ordering all further railways to be laid in narrow gauge. The existing standard gauge had to be pulled up and Anglo Cape narrow gauge laid in its place. London's ruling may have followed on from Queensland's success. It is generally not realised that the colony led the world in its use of Anglo Cape narrow gauge when it began laying the main line to Toowoomba in 1864.

By 1880, South Africa had completely switched to Anglo Cape narrow gauge. Soon after, the dark decade of the Boer War began. During this period the railways were used for defence supply purposes and the fast movement of troops up and down the country. It was not until 1910, well after the Boer War finished, that the South African Railways were established as a united entity to quickly become the largest railway system in Africa.

The 20th century saw huge advances in the transport infrastructure of South Africa. High priority was given to developing highways and freeways, and further extending the rail system, often with electrification. The huge Hexton Tunnels project, one of the great wonders of the world, was completed in 1989, eliminating 6 kilometres of steep grades and sharp curves on the main north–south line. Security concerns and defence requirements drove these developments, particularly into South West Africa where the South West African People's Organisation was leading a fight for independence. (In 1990 South West Africa won its independence to become Namibia.)

Over the Christmas period of 1989, I took myself to South Africa and the protectorate that was to become Namibia for a holiday. Along the way, I also studied the infrastructure of the region and visited Australian peacekeeping troops in Namibia. This was my first trip to that part of the world and I was surprised by the high standards of roads and railways. It was often said at that time, ahead of the release of Nelson Mandela, that South Africa had first world infrastructure in a third world setting. This is still the situation today.

South Africa and the giant South African railways would have been a great anchor for Rhodes' Cape to Cairo railway, but the chances of this happening are less likely today than ever before, as so many countries in Africa remain in political turmoil.

At the time of my first visit, the stand off between the so-called front line states such as Zimbabwe, Zambia, Zaire and Mozambique and South Africa was very real. Many nations had adopted United Nations backed sanctions against South Africa because of its policy of apartheid. Officially Zambia, Zimbabwe and Zaire had done so, but on this visit I discovered an interesting dimension to the relationship. Every twelve weeks, the railway managers of these three nations would secretly meet with the senior railway managers of South Africa Railways to plan the movements of freight to and from the major South African ports.

For all the indignation, the truth was that nothing would be allowed to stop the trains operating. The practical application of these secret meetings could be seen just south of Johannesburg. Here a huge and very modern marshalling yard sorted all the traffic between the front line states and the South African ports of Durban, Port Elizabeth and Cape Town. It was as if the railways could be operated in a cocoon and separate to the political realities of Africa. This arrangement certainly allowed large quantities of food and grain to be shifted inland, thus avoiding famine and death for thousands of people. Today, it does not suit anyone in Southern Africa to highlight these matters, but the role of the railways in that turbulent period of history should be remembered.

During my hectic visit in late 1989, I managed to squeeze in a ride on a freight train out of Windhoek, the very tidy capital of Namibia. It was a warm summer night and there had been some shootings not far from Windhoek in the build up to the ballot for independence. Despite the security concerns, the redoubtable Nick Warner, liaison officer from the Australian Department of Foreign Affairs and Trade, and a couple of Army colonels managed to get me on board.

We climbed steadily out of the main freight yards. I could see a heavy German influence in the architecture of many of the station buildings. (This was not surprising as South West Africa was once a German colony.) The roofs and eaves were very substantial, reflecting more the requirements of a European winter than the hot, dry climate of this part of the world.

The mixed freight train of about 1500 tonnes took us towards Seeheim Junction and ultimately onto South Africa. When we disembarked for some wonderfully cold beers at the Soldiers Canteen Club, I reflected on how significant is was that freight trains were still operating in the lead up to the ballot for independence, especially as rebels were continuing their guerrilla war against the South African armed forces. The trains did keep running and today the Trans Namib operates across Namibia offering a spectacular sunset trip.

In between the railways of North Africa and the railways of South Africa there are many small railway systems using a whole lot of different gauges. Most of these African countries can ill afford their railway systems, many of which were developed to link mining projects in the hinterland to the nearest port.

Arguably, the most famous of the 'middle' lines is the Mombasa to Nairobi metre gauge that links the capital of Kenya to the Indian Ocean. Built at the end of the 19th century, it operates today with varying degrees of success. Romantic passenger train experiences across the equator and the Rift Valley await, but it is container freight traffic that provides the greatest potential.

As the railway was being built, the man-eating lions of Tsavo terrified and ate many construction workers. (Today things are a little safer.) The subject of *The Ghost and the Darkness*, a gripping movie made in 1996, it took considerable determination and courage to complete the bridge over the Tsavo River. Even more determination was required to push the line, which became dubbed the lunatic line, through to Lake Victoria. The splendid coffee-table book *Railway across the Equator* records in wonderful detail how this extraordinary line was built.

Buried away in the *Records and Hansards* of Westminster is the 1896 debate on the Railway Bill that provided for this mammoth project, which was bitterly attacked in parliament. Henry Labouchere read to the House of Commons what might be considered the most accurate railway poem ever written:

What it will cost no words can express,
What is its object no brain can suppose,
Where it will start from no one can guess:
Where it is going to no body knows.
What is the use of it none can conjecture:
What it can carry there's none can define:
And in spite of George Curzon's superior lecture,
It is clearly nought but a lunatic line.

Unlike many African railways, the Mombasa to Nairobi proved its worth and remains fully operational into the 21st century. There are many lunatic lines around the world, but this was not one of them.

As well as a British and German influence on Africa's railways, the Chinese, French and Italians have also played a role.

As a way of exerting a geopolitical influence, in the 1970s China decided to provide a considerable amount of foreign aid to Tanzania and Zambia to help build the Tan–Zam railway. Constructed in Anglo Cape gauge, it was intended that the railway would by-pass South Africa thus allowing Zambian copper to have direct access to the Indian Ocean. The railway has had a chequered history over its first 25 years, with many breakdowns and track failures.

The French colonial influence on the railways was not insignificant. Its colonies, such as Algeria, were heavily under the influence of French railway engineers and French railway companies built and operated many of the railways, which were ultimately built as standard gauge. Station buildings were not unlike some of the best railway buildings in France.

Italy's influence was in establishing a quaint narrow gauge system of 3' 1½" (or 950 mm) in parts of what is now Eritrea and Ethiopa. Against all odds, following the devastating war between Eritrea and

Ethiopa and years of famine, reconstruction of the line from Eritrea's Red Sea port of Mitz'íwa to its capital Asmara has commenced in earnest.

In late 2003, some 52 000 live sheep from Australia were offloaded at Mitz'íwa after they had been stranded for months at sea, the result of a curious rejection of the cargo by Saudi Arabia. Rather than rail being used in the rescue, it was the strong links developed between Eritrea and Australia through the work of the Fred Hollows Foundation in Asmara that helped save the sheep.

No account of the railway realm of Africa would be complete without reference to the famous Blue Train, which runs between Pretoria and Cape Town.

Having been held up in traffic, I almost missed my chance to experience one of the most sensational rail trips available anywhere in the world. I boarded the luxury sleeper just in the nick of time to find a chilled bottle of champagne waiting as a welcome in my cabin. A long and leisurely lunch in the comfortable dining car lasted from Krugersdorp to Kimberley. Having enjoyed too much good company, good food and good wine, I made it back to my cabin in time to change into shorts and runners for our late afternoon arrival at Kimberley, where we were due to stop for about forty minutes. I managed a short jog around the station yards, without veering too far from the train. You never know when there might be a sudden change of timetable!

That evening I joined a group of lively Germans for a stint in the lounge car before a late dinner which was as equally superb as lunch and went long into the night. Rail travel gives you the chance to meet people in a way that can never be matched by air. A couple of years later when visiting Frankfurt, I sought to look up members of this group, 'Helga' in particular, but without success. Perhaps the dictum that friendships made on cruise ships should remain on cruise ships should be applied to trains as well.

We arrived at Touws River and the edge of the Trans Karoo

Plateau in the early light of dawn, and were ready for the descent into Cape Town through the Stellenbosch wineries. The Blue Train effortlessly swept into one of the Hexton Tunnels complete with passing loop, to emerge some thirty minutes later with the sun well up over green fields, in sharp contrast to the desert scenery we left behind at the other end.

All good things must come to an end and on my arrival at Cape Town that happened with a bang. I would be returning to Pretoria on the decidedly downmarket Trans Karoo. It was high summer and I had been allocated a very clean compartment that slept six in fold down bunks, but it had absolutely no airconditioning. This wouldn't have been too bad if what seemed like half the new recruits of the South African Army hadn't boarded my compartment and carriage and drunk and sung their way back to Pretoria.

Sometime during the night we arrived for a lengthy stop at Der Aar. It was still breathlessly hot. As if to remind me of what I once had, both the northbound and southbound Blue Trains arrived with much ceremony, displaying all their luxury. I peered longingly through the lounge car window and cursed that I had got it so wrong. Rule number 1: always book the better class train last, not first!

It was a long trip back. I left South Africa exhausted but also exhilarated by all I had come across on this working holiday to 'deepest darkest Africa'.

Now, when I try to entice my two sons, Harrison and Dominic, into going on bushwalks with me I tell them we are going into 'deepest darkest Africa'. Often enough their rejoinder is, 'Not another Africa again'. There is, however, only one true Africa and it is well worth visiting, especially by train.

The railway realm of Africa has a great deal of potential, notwithstanding the diversity of the separate systems. While Cape to Cairo will probably never be built, the railways will be modernised and developed. Of this I am sure, so long as there is peace and unity across this vibrant continent.

CHAPTER ELEVEN
CHINA, INDIA, RUSSIA, JAPAN: CURIOUS CONNECTIONS

Over the years, Harbin in north-east China has been well known as a place of secrets and spies. It is less well known for the unique fact that no less than three separate railway empires—Russia, Japan and China—have dominated and controlled this vital hub city.

Just over 100 years ago, when Czar Nicholas II and the Russian government were building the world's longest transcontinental railway from Moscow to Vladivostok, Russian railway engineers saw an opportunity to take a huge short cut across the relatively flat lands of north-east China, thus making considerable savings on both distance and cost for their giant railway venture. Russian diplomats persuaded a weakened Manchu dynasty in Peking that this would be in everybody's interest.

A concession was granted to the Russians at much the same time as other railway concessions were granted to British, French, Belgian, German and even Turkish interests. To some extent, the Russians had earnt the right to this concession by their willingness to help put down the Boxer Rebellion in 1900.

The Russians wasted no time in building the railway across their concession, turning much of that part of China into a defacto Russian colony, most notably at Harbin. The Russian Army was on hand to ensure there were no delays.

Harbin grew rapidly. Mara Moustafine details in her excellent book, *Secrets and Spies: The Harbin Files*, how the Chinese, Russians and large Jewish population, known as the 'Harbintsi', lived reasonably happily together. All this changed in 1917 with the Russian Revolution. Moscow established tight control over Harbin by sending out political officers and the KGB. Under Stalin's policies, many Harbin residents were persuaded to return to Russia or go to Siberia to develop forlorn agricultural projects.

Even when the Russians subsequently built the much longer route in 1915 via Khabarovsk, thus avoiding China, Harbin's role was not entirely reduced. The Russian railways still passed through the city for another 20 years. Then, in 1935, the Japanese invaded Manchuria.

For a number of reasons, including strategic, the Japanese converted the Russian broad gauge to Stephenson standard gauge. The short-cut corridor from Moscow to the Pacific was no longer available to the Soviet Empire. It was the Japanese who now held sway. Times had become very tough for the minority groups in Harbin. The remaining Harbintsi were faced with the choice of either returning to Russia, or heading further south into China and by this means migrating elsewhere around the world.

Harbin railway station became the scene for many sad and gripping farewells as the exodus gathered pace. Sadly, the vast majority of Harbintsi who returned to Russia were regarded with great suspicion by Joseph Stalin and the brutal head of the secret police, Pavlovich Beria. They were automatically branded Japanese spies as tensions built up to World War II.

The long train trip from Harbin to Moscow was too often a trip to summary arrest, trumped up charges, stacked trials and torture. Mara Moustafine records one of the last chilling entries in her cousin's papers: 'to be shot'. The subsequent entry, the date of this young dentist's execution, had been signed by Beria. A few of the Harbintsi were sentenced to slave camps in Siberia. This entailed yet another long train trip in extremely harsh conditions and then usually death by deprivation.

Top: This photo of a pre Ghan passenger train near Marree in South Australia was taken by Reverend John Flynn (Flynn of the Inland) in the early 1920s. (National Library of Australia)
Bottom: This double-stacked freight train is on the Port Augusta to Perth section of Australia's east–west transcontinental railway just out of Port Augusta. The Flinders Ranges are in the background. (GRMS Media)

Opposite top: With Duncan Beggs and Bruce McGowan during a track inspection of the Great Larapinta Grade in September 2003. *Opposite Bottom:* This is where the track from Adelaide to Alice Springs stopped just 1 kilometre outside of Alice. It is also the point from where the new line to Darwin took off. *Top:* The final welding of the new track with the old track at Alice Springs, creating Australia's south–north transcontinental train line. *Bottom:* This original Krupp rail was found lying in the undergrowth near the old Northern Australia Railways formation. (John Kirk, Beyond Images, 2004)

Top: A cheeky pre–dawn check of the gauge just prior to the final clip being put in place. *Bottom:* Former Darwin mayor Ella Stack putting in place the 8 millionth Pandrol clip. *Opposite top:* Waving off the first freight train from Adelaide to Darwin, wearing the regulation safety vest. (Jonathan Thomas and Railway Digest) *Opposite bottom:* The first freight train was hauled out of Adelaide to Alice Springs by a locomotive painted with the central Australian motif, the Purna.

Opposite top: The Pichi Richi steam train, on parallel narrow gauge track, chasing our freight train just past Stirling North. People gathered along the entire length of track cheering 001 on its journey to Darwin. *Opposite bottom:* The magnificent arc of that first freight train as it travelled north. (John Phillips, Insite Video Productions) *Top:* In the driver's compartment of 001. (John Phillips, Insite Video Productions) *Bottom:* Working the phones in the media centre on 001. (John Phillips, Insite Video Productions)

Opposite top: The first group to travel by train from Adelaide to Darwin. At the marker point of the 1 millionth sleeper were (from left to right): Mike Wilde, Trevor Kennelwell, John Phillips, Malcolm Kinnaird, Ian Parry, Tim Fischer, Bruce McGowan and Rob Heinrichs. (John Phillips, Insite Video Productions) *Opposite bottom:* The troublesome observation car that shut down the airconditioning during the hottest part of the trip. (John Phillips, Insite Video Productions) *Top:* There was a great buzz of excitement at Adelaide on departure. (Jonathan Thomas and Railway Digest) *Bottom:* The enthusiastic crowd at Katherine waiting for the arrival of the first freight train through town. (John Phillips, Insite Video Productions)

Opposite top: With my wife Judy just before we departed Adelaide on the first Ghan through to Darwin. (Tom Roschi Photography) *Opposite bottom:* In our cabin on The Ghan. *Above:* The Ghan with the beautiful MacDonnell Ranges in the background. (John Kirk, Beyond Images, 2004)

Opposite: According to one version of history, The Ghan was originally named after the Afghan camel traders who lived in outback Australia. Here a camel handler meets the new Ghan. (John Kirk, Beyond Images, 2004) *Top:* Following the train lines that cross the main runway at Peshwar airport. *Bottom:* Our welcome at Jamrud railway station just before we joined the steam train that would take us up the Khyber Pass and the 3000 foot grade.

Opposite top: With Pakistani railway officials at Jamrud railway station. We are standing behind a model of the steam train. *Opposite bottom:* The train's guard, in his magnificent blue uniform, at the entrance to the Khyber Pass. *Top:* Gaurding the magnificent steam locomotive that pulled us up the Khyber. *Bottom:* At the first zig zag loop. The Khyber is in the background.

Top: Halfway up the Khyber Pass. The railway to heaven can be seen in the middle ground.
Bottom: Forgoing my usual Akubra, I was presented with this unusual piece of tribal headwear at the Khyber Rifles Officer mess. When this photo was printed in the *Sydney Morning Herald* many people thought I was wearing a loaf of bread.

The lucky Harbintsi were those who decided to head south to Shanghai and on to other parts of the world. Many arrived in Australia. They worked hard and enjoyed prosperity and freedom and brought skills with them often learnt by working on the Harbin railway.

At the end of World War II, the Russians became the occupying force until China, under Mao, finally took control of the Harbin railway corridor in the early 1950s. Today, the railways dominate this rapidly growing part of China, with its heavy-duty standard gauge, high standard electrification and track duplication.

While the Russian railways no longer operate in Manchuria and have been clipped back by the break up of the Soviet Union, they still remain a huge enterprise with 1.5 million employees. For 140 years, the railway systems of both the Russian Empire and subsequently the Soviet Union were, in track distance, by far the largest in the world. For the Trans-Siberian travellers, the distance from Moscow was marked off every 100 metres along the 9000 kilometre route. The railways played a vital role in Russian life. They were just about the only way to get around the country, as motor vehicle ownership was severely restricted under Stalin and later communist leaders.

What the Russian Revolution did do, was produce one of the world's most extraordinary metro systems. While the western world was recovering from the Great Depression, Moscow was building over 200 kilometres of underground track and a set of magnificent stations, with extravagant galleries, corridors and arches complete with chandeliers. One Moscow metro line was built as a true circle. Trains on this line run in one long, gentle curve.

Today, the Russian railways have come under enormous pressure as they try to handle the switch from the command economy to the market economy and meet the grossly inflated payroll bill from a shrinking revenue base. Gradually, productivity is being lifted and maybe the worst of the contraction of freight tonnages is over. Coal continues to dominate rail freight, with well over 200 million tonnes carried annually. Passenger journeys are on the decline, but the main routes, such as that from Moscow to St Petersburg, are being upgraded complete with an attempt to mount a fast train service.

To ride a train in Moscow today and visit one of the main railway stations is a disappointing experience. The somewhat run down system has seen far better days. The presence of security personnel and soldiers with automatic weapons is a sharp reminder of the violent terrorist attacks that have occurred in Moscow in recent years.

The question remains as to why Czar Nicholas I adopted the curious, but neat, five foot broad gauge and not the Stephenson standard gauge that was being laid in Europe at the time. The role of the engineer George Washington Whistler has to be part of the reason. Whistler, who built multi-gauge railways in the United States, travelled to Russia in 1842 to construct the railway from Moscow to St Petersburg. His experience of gauges other than standard gauge may have encouraged the Czar to make the strategic decision to create a break of gauge thus limiting Europe's territorial ambitions.

Today, the fastest growing railway system in the world, in terms of track length, number of trains, passenger journeys and freight tonnage is that of China. Like Russia, China has commenced a program of modernisation and restructuring designed to lift the productivity of the more than 3 million people who are on the railway payroll.

Right now, China is building the world's newest and longest branch line, to Lhasa, Tibet. This is, of course, not a transcontinental as it is an internal railway that does not complete a crossing of a continent. The great railway venture is not without controversy, however, as the Tibetans fear that even more Han Chinese will descend upon Lhasa, helping to make the locals a minority in their own sacred city. Nevertheless, with the earthworks already complete, the great train journey from Beijing to Lhasa awaits. All proceeding smoothly, this will be in 2008.

Mao Tse-Tung was a great user of trains. (There is famous film footage of Mao travelling by train with the Dalai Lama on their way to meetings to discuss Tibet.) One of Mao's favourite trips on his special train was to his summer retreat, near Dalian. His experience of train travel would have, no doubt, been very different to that experienced by the vast majority of Chinese.

In many of the bigger stations there were special platforms and lounges for the apparatchik and VIPs. I once asked to visit the Shanghai railway station, causing some chaos when our convoy of vehicles was allowed to drive into the station and down platform one. We were ushered into an extraordinary lounge with huge fish tanks full of exotic fish. I was assured the great Mao had trod the carpet on which I stood. Certainly, there was no indication that new carpet had been laid for some time.

To this day, China's railways continue to operate giant steam engines, although these relics of the last century are now being replaced by diesel locomotives. On arrival in Xian a couple of years ago, I spotted a steam engine working away in the distance and asked if I could visit the railway station to see the locomotive first hand. The very officious young guide replied that it was not possible as China no longer used steam engines. I asked again and said I was willing to wager that there were steam engines operating in Xian that day. After making some phone calls, the guide returned looking a little sheepish. I was right, he conceded. He would be happy to take me to the railway yards.

Xian is my favourite city in China. It is one of the great cities of the Silk Road, famous for its fortified walls with elaborate entry gates, and the army of terracotta warriors still being uncovered in large numbers a little to the east beyond the city walls. A great deal of freight is sorted and handled in the Xian railway yards. I noted on that visit that some consignments had already been on the railways for months waiting to get to their final destination.

The giant black steam engines with over a dozen wheels, including ten giant driving wheels, were very impressive. I subsequently discovered that one of the Five Year Plans following the devastating Cultural Revolution provided for a new steam engine fleet of around 5000 locomotives.

Unfortunately, I did not get to ride the luxurious Marco Polo Express, complete with its very soft class carriages, out of Xian and back to Beijing. In this 'classless' society, the terms hard class and soft class describe very succinctly the difference in comfort levels between the two types of carriages. In hard class, where the proletariat travel, the seats are hard benches without much leg room. In soft class, where the cadres travel, the seats are spacious and generously upholstered and are decorated with doilies and lace cushions.

China did not hesitate to adopt the Stephenson standard gauge when its railways were first established by a British company around 1880 in Shanghai. The railways remain an absolute priority for the Chinese today. While their freeway system is being expanded, this is one realm where trains will remain the dominant method of transport for some time.

In India, the first concession for a railway was granted under the administration of the viceroy, Lord Dalhousie. He stipulated that the main gauge be Imperial broad gauge. However, the cheaper metre gauge system was also laid out, often in direct competition with the broad gauge system. Today, following the massive Unigauge project, just about the entire network runs on Imperial broad.

The giant railway stations of India such as Victoria Station in Mumbai or Hawrah Station in Kolkata (formerly Calcutta) are a kaleidoscope of Indian life. They seem to operate in a state of colourful confusion, but work surprisingly well, particularly if you have a confirmed reservation in your pocket and have secured your berth against all oncomers.

Despite the fact that India has a generous loading gauge, little effort has been made to maximise freight train efficiency by developing double-stacked container operations. Not surprisingly, given their relative wealth, there is a huge gap between the highly computerised container systems in the United States and Australia and the rather historic system of India where labour is so much cheaper. But with India's growing middle class and increasing technological sophistication, the need to boost productivity will bring change.

The Indian railways remain under government ownership and are still very bureaucratic. Each year, the railways carry 5 billion passengers and 500 million tonnes of freight. Each day it operates some 8000 passenger trains, comprising hundreds of long-distance trains as well as regional and suburban services. This represents a mammoth task, on a system with a very poor safety record.

Attempts are being made to rapidly upgrade signalling and the management of trains on single track to reduce accidents and boost rail productivity. The new main line from Mumbai to Goa is as good as it gets in terms of engineering, as it sweeps directly down the coast, cutting off the lengthy inland loops of the old railway. So progress is being made. However, political sensitivities have resulted in costly interventions, particularly over the control of freight rates. This is probably a small price to pay for living in one of the world's biggest democracies.

Buried in the Indian railway system are some delightful tourist and mountain railways, such as the luxurious 'Palace on Wheels', which travels to India's major tourist spots, and the Darjeeling–Himalayan 'toy train' railway. Each summer, this railway carried the colonial officers and their families, together with the wealthy Indians, from the fiercely hot plains to the hill stations in the cool foothills of the Himalayas. Similar mountain railways include the better engineered Simla railway, north of Dehli, and the extraordinary Nlgiri railway. These railways also fulfilled important freight functions, transporting local horticultural produce. They remain very popular today, where and when they operate, with their spectacularly scenic backdrops although there is often the risk of breakdown, leaving passengers stranded halfway up the mountain.

Japan commenced the development of its railways a little later than Europe with the first passenger service operating out of Tokyo in 1872. Its railways were heavily influenced by British railway engineers and operators, who encouraged the use of Anglo Cape gauge. Indeed, the first royal coach for the Emperor of Japan was built in Birmingham and was used by him on that first passenger service from Tokyo.

Like most railway realms, there was ongoing debate about the best gauge to use. There had been some experimentation with Stephenson standard gauge, but in the 1950s, after a fierce debate, Japan decided to adopt it as a completely new gauge. It also introduced the world's first high-speed railway, the Shinkansen, meaning 'new main network'.

This huge project was driven by an incredible man, Shinji Sogo, who was also known as Old Man Thunder. In 1955, the Japanese government turned in desperation to the 71-year-old to lead the recovery of the Japanese railways. Born in 1884, Shinji Sogo had worked for over five decades on the railways of Japan and China, including a one-year exchange to the United States in 1917. He had stood up to the military both in Manchuria in the 1930s and in Japan during World War II. But now his biggest battle lay with convincing the notoriously conservative bureacracy, the cabinet and the parliament of Japan that it was time to be bold.

The more cautious approach would have been to expand the existing narrow gauge to its maximum limits, particularly on the congested Tokyo–Osaka line. While early research had shown the service could be upgraded to provide a five-hour service, Shinji Sogo believed the Shinkansen could cover the same distance on standard gauge in about 2 hours and 40 minutes with streamlined, all electrified train sets on a track that carried no slow trains or freight services.

Sogo was a masterful political operator. Fully aware that there would be a budget overrun, he reduced the estimated costs by half in order to gain Diet approval. Ultimately, the cost of the project was double the original estimate. When finalising the bid and documents for Cabinet and the Diet, Sogo is quoted as saying:

> What you must understand my friend is that not only would the Diet reject an appropriation for Yen 300 billion, but those short sighted politicians would demand that we go back to the less expensive plan to simply improve the narrow gauge system. The standard gauge project would be dead, perhaps forever and our country would be denied an opportunity of a lifetime. If we permit our project to die it would be a great disservice to our country. You and I must not let that happen.[1]

With these famous words, the final submission was put to the Cabinet in July 1958. On 19 December, it finally approved the project to build the Shinkansen. If only the same tactics had been adopted for the Sydney–Canberra–Melbourne Very Fast Train (VFT) project, there may have been a 2 hour 50 minute service between Australia's two largest cities today!

In 1959, with construction of the Shinkansen having commenced, and against all precedent, Shinji Sogo was appointed for a second term as president of the Japanese National Railways. He continued to lead and manage the construction, often making difficult decisions, such as the decision to bypass the city Gifu to save billions of yen and fifteen minutes of travel time. As a result of local fury a compromise was ultimately found, to build a magnificent Shinkansen railway station in the middle of a paddock near Hashima.

As trade minister, I went to Gifu to open an Australian designed housing development. Ambassador Ashton Calvert and Austrade had wisely arranged my travel by train, so after the official lunch we departed from the curiously positioned Hashima station. I recall querying why the station was located in a paddock and was advised ever so diplomatically that this had been the wish of a powerful member of the Diet.

1. Extract from *Old Man Thunder* by Bill Hosokawa, Sogo Way, 1997.

With the huge task almost complete, Shinji Sogo, the father of the bullet train, stepped down as President of the Japanese National Railways in 1963. At 10 am on 1 October 1964, at a spectacular opening officiated by Emperor Hirohito, the first gleaming bullet train from Osaka and Tokyo commenced operation. No reference was made to ex-president Shinji Sogo nor was he allocated a seat in the VIP stand. He was subsequently decorated with one of the highest honours in Japan. Having lived a vigorous 97 years, he died in 1981.

The Shinkansen has been a brilliant success, no doubt helped along by the growth in the Japanese economy in the 1960s and 1970s. Operational profits were huge as was the growth in traffic. The Shinkansen became even faster and the network of high-speed trains expanded. For all of its period of operation there have been no fatalities. Not even earthquakes created too many concerns, as the system operates on a split second shutdown.

On a couple of occasions, I have had the privilege of being able to ride in the cabin of these incredibly punctual trains. With a white-gloved driver in control, I have travelled the new line north of Tokyo into the mountains to step straight from Shinkansen onto a ski lift.

Today, new generation Shinkansen continue to create speed records. Average speeds are well over 200 kilometres per hour. In July 1996, a new generation Shinkansen reached 443 kilometres per hour. The system continues to plan ahead for even faster services.

Japan introduced the world to high-speed rail, utilising conventional but highly engineered track. Despite a decline in the Japanese economy, commitment to the development of public rail infrastructure remains. Japan has continued its investment in an expanding Shinkansen network while developing an ultra-fast Mag-Lev for the Tokyo–Osaka corridor. Despite this, and the fact that Japan has more passenger journeys than most other high-speed systems in the world, it remains to be seen if future economic momentum is sufficient to underpin the costly and many-faceted railway system of Japan.

It is an odd collection of countries—Russia and China, India and Japan. All are committed to their railways. All are modernising their systems in different but exciting ways. All represent a positive future for the railways in the 21st century.

CHAPTER TWELVE

GREATER ASIA: UP THE KHYBER

Marco Polo and, well before him, the armies of Alexander the Great rode through the Khyber Pass heading east. Ghenghis Khan and Kublai Khan headed west through the Khyber Pass, invading all the way to the Danube. As a subaltern Winston Churchill stood guard in the Khyber as did Lawrence of Arabia, Winston before the Great War and leading airman Lawrence well after. Even Margaret Thatcher lunched at the historic Khyber Rifles Officer's mess. Now, I make no claim about belonging to the aforementioned group, but unlike them I can at least say I steamed up the Khyber Pass and on a glorious sunny Sunday!

After three wars between Great Britain and Afghanistan, and long before independence was granted to India and Pakistan, the British made the decision to push the Imperial broad gauge track up the north-west frontier from Lahore to the Khyber Pass. Stopping just short of the Afghanistan border, this presented an enormous set of challenges not only for the engineers, but also for the construction gangs, who occasionally came under attack from tribes in the area. Inspecting this railway many years after it was built gave me a new insight into the strategic and defence advantages of rail.

As my commercial jet touched down at Peshawar airport, the main airport for the region, in 1998, I noticed a set of double track railway lines running right across the runway and, in the distance, two steam engines heading towards the Khyber Pass. This is absolutely unique, a point where steam trains intersect with jet planes. I keep urging Pakistani diplomats to arrange photos of this for tourist promotion but so far without success.

Our party quickly transferred to Jamrud station, the last station on the plains, where a huge banner of welcome was waiting, along with a delegation of Pakistani railway officials and a group from the Australian community in Islamabad. The whole escapade up the Khyber Pass had been organised by Anna Berghauser, a bright-eyed Australian who operated a travel business from Islamabad. She had worked closely with our ambassador Geoff Allen and local head of Austrade, Bill Mahon, to ensure that the Pakistani railways were able to supply this specially chartered steam train.

This was going to be an extraordinary day in a part of the world that has been long fought over, particularly during the period of the 'great game' in the 19th and early 20th centuries when Russia and Britain were dancing with menace in the area. However, the only dancing we encountered that day was of welcome.

The train guards, in their magnificent deep navy blue British-styled uniforms, looked appropriately in control. With a shrill blow of the whistle, we jerked out of Jamrud and were hurled towards the entry to the Khyber Pass, a couple of kilometres to the west. There was a delightful degree of improvisation. Fold-up chairs were used in one of the carriages, but none of this mattered as the giant red and brown walls of the Khyber Pass loomed into view.

The train comprised three passenger carriages, with one steam locomotive in front pulling hard and one steam locomotive at the back pushing hard. I estimated we were doing about 60 kilometres per hour until the single track crossed a magnificent bridge on a gentle curve and the serious climbing began. Suddenly the train came to an abrupt halt. We had entered the first of the zig zags and needed to change the points and back out of the loop onto the higher track.

Now, zig zags can be over-engineered and under-engineered. On the Khyber, the British engineers left nothing to chance with each zig zag having a double loop, allowing trains going up the track to pass trains going down at the reverse point of the zig zag.

As we travelled further into the Pass, which was starting to narrow, I estimated we had climbed 1000 feet from the Peshawar plains in just over an hour. We were now passing small villages and farmhouses, all safely hidden behind huge mud brick walls designed to give some protection against the elements, but also against raiders and guerrilla gangs.

Halfway between two zig zags we stopped for morning tea at a local village. We could have not been more welcomed, and were greeted with singing and dancing by the local children. Two giant kettles and several teapots, which had probably been in use for over a century, produced many cups of very tasty, strong, black tea. Sadly, due to security concerns and many other challenges such as the Pakistani railways' large budget deficits, steam trains up the Khyber Pass operate only sporadically, so our tourist dollars were much appreciated.

With a long blast on the locomotive's whistle, we set off again, working our way through another zig zag from where we could look down on a sentry box of gigantic proportions. This sentry box at a key entrance to the Pass is supposed to have been where Winston Churchill once stood guard. How true this is, one can only guess. Certainly Churchill did serve in India with the Seventh Hussars, taking his bathtub with him, and at one stage he did secure a posting on the north–west frontier.

As we resumed our climb, I spotted the only safety ramp for runaway trains I had ever seen. On a section of track, at the bottom of a steep grade, a set of lonely points led to a very short and very steep branch line that simply headed straight for the sky.[1]

---

1. Recently I was advised that years ago there was a safety rail siding at Tumulla, near Bathurst, on the Sydney–Broken Hill main line. Maybe there are a few more around the world from the period when train braking systems were far from safe.

I asked the driver how the system worked as it appeared that it couldn't be changed automatically. 'Mr Fischer,' came the reply. 'It is really very simple. The trains coming down the pass must be going slow enough for the assistant fireman to be able to jump off, run ahead and change the points from the safety ramp branch line back to the main line. The points are always set to the safety ramp so if a train is out of control or going too fast, it automatically switches to the safety ramp.' I could only respond by saying that in a sense the line was heading directly to heaven without a stop!

We then dived through a couple of tunnels in a very steep and narrow section of the Pass. At one point, where both the road and railway lines squeezed through, it was no wider than the length of a tennis court. Mountains hundreds of metres high soared above us on both sides. Looking down on the road from the train, all I could see were a few cars and a lot of heavily loaded trucks, their engines growling as they climbed.

Only one or two of us, such as the military attache, Group Captain Graeme Carroll, had been through the Khyber Pass before and it was an eye opener for all of us, as it was for the Pakistani railway officials travelling with us. I discussed with them the growth of railway tourism around the world and the uniqueness of the trip they could offer. They were sceptical, and I think overwhelmed by the struggle to maintain existing passenger services with their basic operations. As a government-owned railway in a desperately poor country, the Pakistani railways are very badly run down in many places.

It was now late morning and we were travelling along a plateau, having reached the summit a few kilometres back. We slowed down into the last station. It had five sidings in good condition that had presumably been used to hold troop trains in the past. About a kilometre ahead and much lower down was the fortified border gateway and customs post between Pakistan and Afghanistan. Just to one side of the station stood a military outpost, which had been heavily shelled by the Russians during the 1980s. For good measure some of the empty shells had been mounted on a ceremonial wall.

The Khyber Pass is a place steeped in the blood of countless wars. On this day we noticed the flags of the Taliban flying on the Afghanistan side of the border. They had recently captured this territory all the way back to Kabul, some 200 kilometres distant.

After handing out gifts to the train crew, we jumped into four-wheel drives to be taken to Khyber Rifles Unit of the Pakistan army. In the officer's mess we enjoyed superb and dramatic dancing by five tribes of the north-west frontier, culminating in me being crowned with local head gear, always a hazard for visiting parliamentarians. This is one reason why my broad-brimmed Akubra is so very useful. I can quickly claim it is impossible for me to remove my hat due to medical and cultural reasons!

As we travelled back down the steep-sided Khyber Pass by car, I reflected, just for a moment, on the many ambush sites it had to offer. And when we swerved to miss a horse, I remembered that Queen Victoria had sent four giant Clydesdale horses to Kabul as a peace gesture.

Her gesture made little difference. The three Anglo–Afghan wars resulted in draws at best, but defeat in reality for the British. In a famous retreat from Kabul back towards the Khyber Pass in 1842, 4330 British soldiers and 12 000 camp followers were killed. Only assistant surgeon Brydon survived to tell the tale. If a railway had existed from the Khyber Pass to Kabul, the result might have been very different.

The problems faced by the Pakistani railways are problems faced by railways in developing countries all around the world. These include poor security, lack of capital for much needed modernisation, and massive over-manning. The resulting large losses in turn lead to central governments giving rail even lower priority in budget allocations. Later in the tour I discovered a classic example of this phenomenon when I witnessed the unloading of Australian wheat at a huge port near Karachi. The rail track came right onto the wharf, but there were no bulk wheat wagons. Rather, the 30 000 tonnes of grain was bagged on the wharf, a very slow process. The 3 600 000 bags were then put on open wagons or box cars to be sent up country to the flour mills in the north!

I simply could not believe that a process such as this could still be used at the very end of the 20th century. It was then very gently explained to me that the mills could only receive flour by bags, that bagging the wheat provided work for a very poor population, and that it aided the necessary degree of pilfering for families to survive.

Unlike Pakistan, some of the railway systems in greater Asia are doing very well. The Malaysian and Thai railway systems are a case in point. Dominated by substantial metre gauge networks, with more and more double track and from Kuala Lumpur to Ipoh electrification as well, these railways are pointing the way ahead for some of their neighbours.

Malaysia has also just completed a new standard gauge line from downtown Kuala Lumpur to the magnificent Kuala Lumpur International Airport. Taking less than half an hour to cover nearly 60 kilometres at speeds of around 120 to 160 kilometres per hour, this one-off system is as good as it gets anywhere in the world. It is equal to or better than the new Heathrow–Paddington above-ground service or the Singapore MRT from Changi airport into Singapore city.

Malaysia is making a huge effort to win more freight to rail with a focus on container traffic, particularly from the hinterland to the major ports. The most interesting of these port–rail developments is at the container port of Pelapas, near Jahore, where a new branch line has been built, although in 2003 only one or two trains a week were required for the containers.

Enter the vision of Dr Mahathir, until 2003 the long-serving prime minister of Malaysia, who proposed the ultimate link railway from Southeast Asia through China and Russia to Europe and the United Kingdom. I vividly recall discussing this briefly with him at Brisbane airport in 1996. While the project was not able to be finalised during his period in office, the foundation was laid with upgrading of the main west coast main line from Singapore to Kuala

Lumpur, Ipoh, Butterworth and into Thailand. It was envisaged that the existing metre gauge main line through Hua Hin to just near Bangkok would then be used. There were several options under consideration for the link to China.

One option involved the controversial re-opening of a section of the Thai–Burma death railway, which was built by Japanese prisoners of war during World War II, including such notable Australians as Sir John Carrick, Weary Dunlop and Tom Uren. The link would then be made utilising existing Burmese railway lines through the north-east into China and Kunming.

Another option involved travelling through the north-east of Thailand to the Australian-built Friendship Bridge over the Mekong River to Vientiane and then due north through Laos to Kunming. This is by far the best option. In fact, Australian engineers have already built a centre line along the bridge, capable of carrying metre gauge rail track.

The Friendship Bridge was aptly named as its traffic does indeed get very close. On the Laotian side traffic travels on the left-hand side of the road; on the Thai side it travels to the right. I once asked a former Thai prime minister just how the bridge would actually work. He replied with a smile, 'No problems. We will simply build a hospital at either end of the bridge!'

A third option for Dr Mahathir's railway involved going through Cambodia and Vietnam. While this might be more favourably viewed politically, particularly in ASEAN forums, it is a much longer route and would involve several costly new bridges.

It remains to be seen whether or not the mighty Mekong link railway will be completed this century, especially as Dr Mahathir's successor has cancelled an important upgrade project in Malaysia. I remain hopeful, even though freight and passengers will have to switch to standard gauge at Kunming for the trip across China. Then at the Russian border a switch will have to be made to Czar broad gauge, and finally at the Polish border a further switch will be required back to standard gauge for the run through Europe. It will take a lot of vision, purpose and leadership before the first trains run right through from downtown Singapore to Stockholm or Edinburgh.

Singapore's long-distance train station, from which such journeys might start, is owned and operated by the Malaysian railway system under an extraordinary 999 year lease. There is ongoing debate between these not always friendly neighbours over whether or not the station should be upgraded or banished to the edge of Singapore. If Malaysia does not cut off Singapore's extra water supply (which comes by a viaduct from Jahore) then perhaps Singapore will not cut off Malaysia's main line. After having been married in the 1960s, Singapore and Malaysia sometimes act a bit like jealous divorcees.

The other railway systems of greater Asia, which by any reasonable definition must include the Middle East and Turkey, are also considering modernisation as they face huge problems of passenger and freight congestion.

Lines such as that from Ad Dammam to the Saudi Arabian capital Riyadh are built to a very high standard. Station security is also of a high standard as I can attest after having been nearly arrested at Ad Dammam railway station after trying to take a photo of the Australian-made BHP steel rails that were used for the tracks. While I was allowed to keep my camera, my film lies crushed in the ground somewhere near the entrance to the station.

It was once possible to travel by the same gauge train from Istanbul right through Iraq to Baghdad. Today you can only dream about this, let alone travelling on further into the extensive Iranian railway system. When there is sustainable peace across the Middle East, the railways in this troubled part of the world will expand again. While we may not see the restoration of the rack and pinion track from Beirut to Damascus over two massive snow-capped mountain ranges, it is more than likely that a line will run from Damascus through Medina to connect with the Saudi Arabian system, ending up at the port of Ad Dammam.

Despite the turmoil in the Middle East, attempts are being made to connect some of the Gulf railways. A few years ago Iran joined its main line system to that of Turkmanistan and the other 'stans' in the Confederation of Former Soviet states. Iran is gradually overcoming years of war with Iraq, and it has certainly built a large modern station on the edge of the ancient city of Eşfahãn. When I visited this station recently as a tourist after leaving parliament, I had trouble gaining entry to the beautiful main hall. I could see several passenger trains waiting at platforms but in a strange vista of contradiction there were no passengers, anywhere. Passenger services had been suspended indefinitely. This is a tragedy, particularly as the Tehran to Eşfahãn line via Qom would make a wonderful daylight tourist train service.

There is a final experience to relate for this realm, an incident that happened in Burma on the Mandalay to Rangoon overnight train. It had been a long haul in a shared cabin of six berths. The old carriage swayed wildly along the run down track, notwithstanding the very slow speed at which it was travelling. A young boy riding on the roof lost his footing and fell to his death. A hessian bag was found, and the boy's body tossed into it to be dispatched to somewhere unknown. The train quickly resumed its journey south. Such accidents not only seemed to happen often, but to be of little consequence. Had this occurred in a place like Melbourne, a full-scale investigation would have been undertaken, a stark reminder of the struggles for life in the developing world.

As well as being crammed with passengers, the carriages on this train were filled with sacks of smuggled goods. Whenever the train slowed down as we approached Rangoon, these sacks were dropped out the windows. Picked up by relatives and associates, they quickly vanished into the nearby streets. I was advised that the goods all came from China and beyond and that for once, I should not ask too many questions.

As we took off from Rangoon International Airport at the

northern end of the city, I spotted the quaint Round Rangoon circle railway with a small passenger train inching its way along the run down track. Sadly, it has to be said, Burma, like its railways, is going around in slow circles.

CHAPTER THIRTEEN
THE TOP TWELVE GRAND STATIONS

All things considered, dimensions, diversity and dignity are all key ingredients in determining my choice of the top twelve railway stations in the world.

Despite the demands for both improved security and levels of cleanliness, railway stations around the world still seem to attract the underbelly of life. While prostitutes have been moved on from London's Picadilly Circus, for example, drug trading still takes place under the nose of the police. So many stations are run down to be almost beyond repair, but not the top twelve I will now detail. I concede that I am both judge and jury in drawing up the list, so hasten to add the only correspondence that will be entered into is perhaps the polite email.

In many ways the top twelve are larger than cathedrals and temples. In all cases, they act as the lynchpin for the railway system they serve. In one sense they are the twelve apostles for the railways of the future as they have been renovated and, in some cases, expanded to cater for a whole new generation of ultra modern, often very high-speed trains.

In making the selection I realise that the grand stations in Germany, the Netherlands and Hungary are deserving of consideration. If Argentina does not make progress in upgrading the Retiro station complex, then clearly one or two of the giant stations of Germany will press their claims to be in the list. The Frankfurt am Main hauptbahnhof is the closest runner up, given its sweeping lines and almost overbearing dignity.

At the risk of offending many, I have carefully considered the claims of over 50 large stations, many of which I have had the good fortune of visiting on the ground, above ground or below ground. In some cases the historic role of the station has been a decisive factor in my decision, in other cases it has been the upgrading of the station to cater to modern needs of increasing numbers of passengers. Based on some very subjective opinions, the twelve grand railway stations I've settled on are: Sydney Central, the Retiro complex in Buenos Aires, Kuala Lumpur Sentral, Victoria Station in Mumbai, Gare du Nord and Gare de Lyon in Paris, Milan Central, Atocha Station in Madrid, St Pancras in London, Bristol Temple Meads, Grand Central in New York and Washington Union Station.

Sydney Central station might seem a biased choice but it is, in fact, a grand old lady. Constructed out of local sandstone, it has a set of deep, underground secrets, including the ghost platforms numbers 26 and 27. Built in the 1970s and accessible through an unmarked door, these platforms are perfectly shaped but have never been visited by a train as the tracks have yet to be laid and electric overhead wiring installed. The theory is that they stand ready to service a new line to Sydney's northern beaches or Sydney–Canberra–Melbourne high-speed trains.

I suppose it is useful to have some surplus capacity already in place for possible future usage. In the meantime, the other 25 platforms give sterling service day in and day out for every kind of passenger train, including the Indian Pacific to Perth, the XPT services to Brisbane, Dubbo and Melbourne and a range of regional commuter and local suburban services. There are a few remaining services to smaller distant centres, such as to Broken Hill, Griffith and Moree, but this is a far cry from the days when the North Coast Mail, North-west Mail, the

Coonamble Mail, the Forbes Mail, the Temora Mail and the South-west Mail dominated overnight services. On special occasions the Sydney Central grand concourse is used as a ballroom and as a special exhibition space. Today, it is much cleaner than it has ever been, and from the main concourse there is now access to the light rail or tramways service to Darling Harbour and inner city suburbs beyond.

One winter Saturday evening my family and I were caught in the buzz of this bustling station as we watched tens of thousands of green and gold bedecked Australian rugby union fans make their way to a big test match at Olympic Park. They were joined by Sydney Swans fans proudly wearing their team colours of red and white on their way to a match at the Sydney Cricket Ground. As we enjoyed the bustle and the colour, a special diesel hauled vintage train, operated by a 3801 locomotive, swept past the platforms and into the underground system to gain access to the Sydney Harbour Bridge.

There is much to enjoy at Sydney Central, helped greatly by the fact it was built to take advantage of the improved design and construction techniques of the late 19th century and the extra space offered by the resumption of an old cemetery on the site. It is not generally realised that the original terminus of the New South Wales Government Railways was built at Redfern, a temporary terminus that served for twenty years. A second Sydney station was then built near the separate and magnificent Sydney mortuary station. Ultimately this station, and the huge hay shed that formed part of the railway yards, grew to a dozen or so platforms during its 30 years of activity. It soon became necessary to contemplate further expansion.

As detailed by John Oakes in his booklet *Sydney's Central*, the bold decision was made to build Sydney Central (the third station) closer to the city proper with a capacity to handle both terminating country and interstate trains as well as through electric suburban trains. Officially opened in 1906, Sydney Central is not only the biggest station in the southern hemisphere, it has platforms on three different levels.

With its cleverly designed flyover junctions (more often called flying junctions) for suburban trains and switchover junctions for all non-suburban inter-urban and long-distance trains, it is well set for its next 100 years. The tram level was also well designed decades ago and, after a break of 30 years, is back in use with modern light rail. We can thank the Sydney Olympics for a recent clean up and upgrade including the installation of lifts and extra access for all suburban platforms.

Also in the southern hemisphere is the Retiro station complex, which includes the Belgrano station (a huge stone building that dominates downtown Buenos Aires) and adjoining Mitre and St Martin stations. The Mitre and Belgrano have a symmetrical concourse framed by colonial-style arches and sit immediately alongside the small third station, St Martin.

Sadly, the Mitre, the terminus for the Imperial broad gauge trains, such as the Tukeman Mail, has seen better days. It must have once been an awe-inspiring sight, like so many of the other major buildings of Buenos Aires. The Colon opera house nearby certainly is and according to Joan Sutherland, it is one of the world's greatest opera houses. The hard times that have befallen Argentina in recent years have caused a deterioration in these buildings, but I have every confidence that the Retiro complex will enjoy a new era of excellence.

Moving northwards just across the equator, I have selected one of the world's newest stations, the steel and glass dominated main station at Kuala Lumpur, known as Sentral. It caters for local suburban trains, as well as the metre gauge system from Singapore through Kuala Lumpur to Georgetown and the Thai border.

In addition, Kuala Lumpur Sentral has a standard gauge connection for the 160 kilometre per hour service to Kuala Lumpur International Airport. This service is tailor made for international passengers with heavy baggage; it is clean and comfortable, swift and spacious and easy to use. Baggage can actually be booked in at the downtown Sentral station and not seen again until you arrive at your final destination.

Critics would say Sentral is too modern to be added to the list of top twelve railway stations of the world. It certainly has dimension and diversity and, no doubt, will develop a degree of dignity with time. It does point the way to the future. The once overcrowded, beautiful, old colonial main terminus looks deserted these days, although it is still used as a suburban station.

There is no doubt Victoria station in Mumbai (previously Bombay) is very much deserving of being selected in the top twelve although, like so many buildings of its era, Victoria station requires a good spring clean to bring out the best in its ornate décor. Charles Sheppard points out in his recent book, *Railway Stations: Masterpieces of architecture*, just how extraordinary this 115-year-old station is.

Designed by consulting architect FW Stevens, the Gothic lines that dominate the exterior of the station stand in stark contrast to a superb central dome inside. On top of the dome is a 5 metre statue of a woman with a torch in her hand, denoting progress. The dome has been struck by lightning over the years; in 1969 a severe lightning strike caused considerable damage. The statue is definitely not of Queen Victoria. If it had been, it might have been toppled years ago in the campaign for independence.

Today, the official name of the station is Chhatrapati Shivaji terminal, although it is still known as Victoria station or VT to its friends. I recall being ushered upstairs into the station master's office during one visit to VT. There were people everywhere, mostly station staff. Everybody there was aware of everybody else's rank, with the station master commanding absolute respect. He was even saluted as we made our way along the many corridors to his office.

The pecking order of Indian society is also reflected in the station concourse. In the course of an hour you can see the whole range of Indian society from the poorest of the poor whose life belongings are bundled in plastic bags to the Indian upper classes with their retinues of servants and luggage bearers.

Europe presents some real challenges to narrowing down the selection. For example, Budapest's West station is a delicious combination of bricks and turrets at either end and a giant steel and glass canopy in between. Then there is the almost grotesque Amsterdam Central station from which the city's canals and streets seem to radiate. In the end, I have selected two from Paris, Gare du Nord and Gare de Lyon, as well as Atocha in Madrid and the giant survivor of World War II, Milan Central.

Gare du Nord has a supreme symmetry attaching to its design. While some contend that Gare du Nord is related to St Pancras in London, having been built at the same time, it will soon have a very direct link when the Eurostar Paris–London service commences with trains running directly between the two stations.

Gare du Nord is a great gateway to Paris. When originally built in the middle of the 19th century, it was located on the edge of the city. Today it is inner city. Even though it is approaching its 150th anniversary, the vision of original architects and engineers meant that it was not difficult to adjust this huge station complex to deal with growth, including the expansion of underground services, such as the RER to Charles de Gaulle Airport, changes to platforms to accommodate high-speed international train services and the extra security needed for Eurostar.

Gare du Nord is not too far from the famous night club, Moulin Rouge, with its windmill and dancing girls, or the magnificent church, Sacré Coeur. Heading out of the station you have a choice of going up the hill to church or down the street to the night life and red light districts. Before you ask, I have done both over the years.

A little different in design, but again featuring a huge overarching and visually uplifting roof is Gare de Lyon, the historic terminal for the first TGV. The French postal service also runs its distinctive bright yellow TGVs out of this station every night. Gare de Lyon is home to the famous Le Train Bleu restaurant. Many railway stations have lost their dining rooms and refreshments rooms, to be replaced with fast food outlets and 'microwave mash'. 'Le Train Bleu' remains a marvellous exception.

This bustling restaurant with a joyful Parisian atmosphere is dominated by thick velvet curtains and cuisine of excellence. You actually get a meal when you order a main course and don't have to produce a microscope to eat the so-called delights of nouvelle cuisine. My first attempt at taking my wife Judy to this great restaurant was a dismal failure. We were on our honeymoon and had tried to fit too much in to one bitterly cold day in Paris. Let me recall with some very carefully chosen words: our communication skills were not fully established at the time! Our second attempt was much more successful.

However, even these two large Paris stations are dwarfed by Milan Central, a creation of Benito Mussolini. Built between the two world wars, its roof is divided into three sets of giant arches with a massive construction of columns and statues and oversized porticos. It is a main junction for rail routes north, south, east and west, many of them international services through the Alps to Geneva and Zurich and Germany.

The main entrance is almost too big to comprehend. In no way can it be said to be subtle or delicate in style, rather it is a giant testimony to a period of Italian excess. Nevertheless, the station works and works well. As home to many of Italy's major businesses, Milan is seen primarily as a business destination. However, it deserves to be recognised as a tourist destination as well with its incomparable Duomo, La Scala Opera House and the elegant Galleria. This 19th century wrought iron-framed glass retail complex has unfortunately not been enhanced by the golden arches of a certain fast food outlet. Milan is also the home of Leonardo da Vinci's painting 'The Last Supper', now restored to all its glory. Milan certainly is a European political, industrial, transport and arts hub.

Atocha station in Madrid is on the list because of a very successful renovation. The introduction of high-speed trains from Madrid to Seville resulted in the need to introduce standard gauge platforms on a new level separate to the Iberian broad gauge and local suburban platforms. In a brilliant display of mouth-watering architectural extravagance, the old train sheds were converted into a huge public concourse complete with restaurant and rainforest framed by a centreline of glass roof. I vaguely recall going to Atocha one morning for a pick-me-up cup of coffee after a big night out. The slightly humid atmosphere, the strong coffee and relaxing ambience of the fully grown palm trees softened my hangover and gave me renewed energy for the program that lay ahead. So, to Madrid must go the prize for the best modern station make-over, although it is slightly let down by the cheapest white plastic chairs you would ever encounter anywhere.

Sadly in March 2004 Madrid's railways were hit by ten separate bombs during morning rush hour. Two hundred people were killed and hundreds more injured. One corner of the Atocha concourse was turned into an emergency hospital and the other into a temporary morgue. The following day and night thousands upon thousands of Spaniards marched in pouring rain to give support to the victims and to express their strength in the fight against terrorism. Many laid wreaths and stood in silence in front of Atocha station.

The station was back in business one day later. It stands tall and proud despite the bombings. Terrorism seems destined to be a regular and ugly part of life in the 21st century. However, we should remember this is not a new phenomenon. In 1962, Paris was put under siege when the OAS, a right-wing group of French army officers opposed to Algerian independence, carried out a series of bomb attacks in the French capital. In 1973 the Irish Republican Army exploded two bombs at London railway stations while in 1980 Bologna railway station was destroyed and hundreds of people killed and injured in a Red Brigade attack.

In the United Kingdom there are many extraordinary railway stations, large and small. On reflection and by the narrowest of margins I have settled on just two, St Pancras in London and Bristol Temple Meads.

St Pancras is really a giant hotel with offices and a massive clock-tower, and a huge traditional one-arch roofed platform area. The hotel of Victorian Gothic design was meant to take out competitors at nearby Euston and Kings Cross stations.

Completed in 1869, Gilbert Scott designed the facade, hotel and office building, while WH Barlow is credited with the great train hall which, like Sydney Central, has its own secrets. As Hamilton Ellis records in *The Pictorial Encyclopedia of Railways*, beneath the platforms catacombs were built to store in a cool atmosphere large quantities of beer and other products from the Midland.

Like many stations around the world, St Pancras is undergoing a complete make-over for the new generation of high-speed trains, in this case the Eurostar services from Paris and Brussels. The approach tracks have been reshuffled, the platforms altered, and the platform roof extended creating some interesting engineering challenges. Charles Sheppard records that in the mid 19th century the huge covered area was built without any support columns, the roof arches springing some 74 metres across all the platforms, with a height of 30 metres at its apex.

St Pancras has a great deal of dignity. The test will be to see if the new extensions blend with the splendour of the past while still remaining operational.

It is hard to go past London's Paddington, Waterloo and Victoria stations, or even the great curved platforms of York, but my other selection for Britain must be the historic Bristol Temple Meads.

Isambard Kingdom Brunel, engineer of the Great Western Railway, was determined to see an edifice built that would make a mark. The Tudor-style facade exists to this day but the layout of Bristol Temple Meads has had many changes since the Brunel broad gauge first arrived from London on 14 June 1841. His original timber roofing had to be replaced, another level was built with the arrival of Midland Railways' standard gauge in 1853 and, later, a curved platform was constructed for through traffic from London to Dawlish and Penzance. For about 40 years this station was the biggest dual gauge station in the world. Of course all of the broad gauge was ripped out and replaced by standard gauge between 1890 and 1892.

All things considered, Bristol Temple Meads deserves its place in the sun, even if the sun does not shine all that often in this part of the Old Dart and even if main line electrification is yet to arrive in Bristol.

The final two selections to make the list of twelve grand stations of the world have to be Grand Central in New York and Washington Union.

At its zenith, cathedral-like New York Grand Central had more than 60 platform tracks arranged on two levels beneath the giant concourse and atrium. With the elimination of steam trains, all the platform and approach areas could be safely roofed and were effectively taken underground. While many of those tracks are no longer used, Grand Central is as splendid today as it ever was, unlike its sister Pennsylvania station, which became sadly seedy when it was modernised and taken underground. Today there is a campaign to restore the pink marble concourse walls that once made Pennsylvania station so grand.

The current Grand Central terminal is the second station on the site, but I suspect one that is going to last for centuries. For those who like oysters, its oyster bar is a famous rendezvous spot where commuters can tuck into a wonderful selection of bivalves and clam chowders as they wait for their Long Island services. While the long-distance trains no longer leave from New York Grand Central, the main building and precinct were heritage protected following a successful campaign spearheaded by Jacqueline Kennedy.

Just three hours to the south by the high-speed Acela, which leaves from Pennsylvania station, is Washington DC's giant Union station. Washington Union is a good football kick away from the United States Congress building and about twenty minutes' walk from the White House. In many ways, Washington Union is not unlike Milan Central with the same dominant light grey colourings and the oversized columns, statues and trimmings. It is said that everything is bigger in the United States but I suspect Milan might be just a shade bigger than Washington. Certainly both are very busy stations serving millions of passengers every year.

I once escaped from my ministerial entourage at Washington Union station after having been in their close company for several days of hectic travelling. We had completed a round of meetings in the Congress building, and I had an hour to spare before a media conference at the Australian Embassy nearby. To the absolute consternation of the accompanying officials, I had the driver pull over at Union station. I jumped out, yelling back that I wanted a break.

I wandered around the main concourse and looked for a train souvenir shop. I bought a book on President Nixon and Watergate, then caught a taxi to the embassy with five minutes to spare. I was not going to miss out on a short break of freedom!

While one becomes cynical as one ages, each one of these stations has left an impression on me. On return visits they still excite me. They are all different, and they are all worth a visit in their own right, but particularly so when they are the starting point for a superb train journey to a destination of interest.

My search for the great stations will continue as stations modernise and revamp themselves, thereby entering a claim or two to be considered in the list of the top twelve stations of the world.

PART THREE

DARWIN AT LAST

CHAPTER FOURTEEN
FIRST FREIGHT TRAIN TO DARWIN

The first freight train to Darwin arrived in Alice Springs early on Friday 16 January 2004. It was one of those blazing hot and clear mid-summer days but without the furnace winds and dust to add to the burden. Two hours later, with ceremonies complete, the FreightLink service, unofficially designated 001, had completed its shunting and was ready for departure on the new section of northbound track and its journey on the world's newest transcontinental railway.

The Great Larapinta Grade loomed just ahead and around the corner. With its 15 kilometre 1 in 83 climb out of Alice Springs towards Tennant Creek, this is the steepest section of track between Alice Springs and Darwin. Would the first train make it smoothly up the grade in the heat without a locomotive breakdown? Would the track withstand pounding by the first proper train to use it, other than small work trains, without buckling?

Not only was it very hot and dry in the early afternoon of this historic day, but the red rocks of the MacDonnell Ranges glowed with radiated heat. In the distance the ranges changed colour to a shimmering dark blue hue, a reflection of the clear skies overhead.

With South Australian premier Mike Rann and Northern Territory chief minister Clare Martin waving the train off, we effortlessly switched over to the world's newest transcontinental. A crowd of thousands shared the joy.

The deep roar of the FreightLink locomotives could be heard as the 1.1 kilometre long, 82 container freight train of over 1600 tonnes gathered momentum. We passed the trail bike area on the north-west edge of Alice Springs where I had briefly got lost only a year before. As we pounded north heading for the huge Cutting No. 5 and climbing steadily, I realised that this was it. At last we were on the new metals, Malcolm's Metals, the rails named after Asia Pacific Transport president, Malcolm Kinnaird.

The previous day in Adelaide it had been my privilege to chair the departure ceremony for 001 at the request of the South Australian government. In planning for the event in liaison with the South Australian government protocol section, FreightLink and Pacific National, who operate the terminal, I had noticed a large open-spaced paddock just outside the freight terminal fence. I suggested this would be a great area to invite the public and this had been agreed. When I arrived just after 7.00 am on the day of the ceremony I discovered a sweeping set of scaffold tiered seating but it was completely empty.

Deeply worried, I wondered if these seats would be filled in time, joking with protocol chief Dean Dempsey that both our heads would roll if only a handful of people turned up. My worries soon evaporated as large numbers of people surged in. There was a great buzz of expectation.

Media activity also built up quickly. I did an early morning live cross from the freight terminal to the Nine Network's *Today* show. It was a very positive, although difficult, interview as it is never easy looking straight down the camera lens talking to somebody thousands of miles away.

As the steady stream of VIP guests began arriving I discovered, to my horror, that a decision had been made to split the speeches and celebrations. One round of speeches was to be in the grand tent away from the public but with the media present. A second round of the same speeches was to be made outside the tent in front of the public. As designated master of ceremonies I accepted my adjusted running sheet with a taut smile and immediately retired to the nearest port-a-loo to quickly adjust my cue cards so I would have two sets of remarks that would sound spontaneous, interesting and, above all else, not repetitive.

I then moved quickly to the stage and called for order. The large crowd inside the tent moved forward to watch proceedings. The speeches from Mike Rann, Clare Martin, federal finance minister Nick Minchin and Halliburton president David Lesar were all up-beat, and made comparisons to the Snowy Mountains scheme, the giant engineering task undertaken some 50 years before.

To end this section of proceedings on a high note, I then made the mistake of calling for three cheers for the world's newest transconti-nental. Alas, a section of the crowd outside heard the cheers and proffered the odd boo. Clearly, they were less than amused that the speeches in the tent had been out of sight of the public.

As we watched the last ceremonial container from Northern Territory Freight Services being loaded onto the train, Bill Gibbins from the container forwarder FCL strolled over and whispered to me that there had been a mishap—the refrigeration container was the wrong way around and would not fit. The red-faced truck driver had to back off, place the container on the ground, swap sides, reload and, second time around, neatly click it into place at the front of the freight wagons. When I explained this to the crowd there was a spontaneous round of applause.

All was ready for departure. I still had to introduce the speakers to address the public from a small stage in front of the train. They all gave shortened versions of their previous speech, but with plenty of energy. The crowd responded warmly.

Texan David Lesar was particularly forthright and well briefed. He was not showing any signs of stress from revelations in the United States about Halliburton's financial arrangements with the Pentagon.

As is often the best way, he took on the critics with direct answers and some counter-attack public relations. Luckily no United States media was present in Adelaide.

The three locomotives had been checked and were now connected to the crew cars and the independent power unit car, which in turn had been connected to the wagons containing the first 82 containers to travel by rail to Darwin.

I yelled out 'All aboard' several times and waved the green flag at the direction of FreightLink and the Australian Railway Group (ARG), the train operators. The waiting firefighting units sent up a fine spray of water. (Two days later the *Adelaide Advertiser* ran a letter saying the railway was okay but the firefighters' celebratory spray had been a waste of water!)

The train gathered pace, stopping briefly at Dry Creek to drop off some of the media. Hundreds of people lined either side of the adjoining Irish broad gauge track and station platforms, right through to the very outskirts of Adelaide. This augured well for a splendid set of ceremonies at Port Augusta, Alice Springs, Tennant Creek, Katherine and then Darwin.

I settled into the centre section of the crew car with Malcolm Kinnaird and Bruce McGowan from Asia Pacific Transport (APT), Rob Hinrichs from Telstra, Ian Parry from EDI (the firm that built the locomotives), cameraman John Phillips and *National Geographic* reporter Simon Worrall. As the lucky seven non-crew on this trip we were given a comprehensive briefing from the FreightLink network manager Mike Wilde and the ARG train manager Trevor Kennelwell, particularly in relation to safety. We were told that it was necessary to wear safety boots and the bright red FreightLink vests at all times when getting on and getting off the train. We were also told that absolutely no alcohol was allowed in or near the locomotives. In addition, it was advised that no alcohol should be consumed for eight hours before joining the locomotives. This was designed to be fair to the drivers.

Soon enough, on an informal roster basis, I joined the others to prepare the pre-packed lunch from Qantas catering. The meal was substantial and excellent, but best remain a secret for fear it will start a precedent on all FreightLink crew cars! Suffice to say, it was important that we were well nourished for the long journey that lay ahead.

This section of the main line from Adelaide to Port Augusta and then on to Tarcoola junction is all controlled by the Australian Rail Transport Corporation (ARTC) from a first floor room at Adelaide's interstate railway station. Whoever was on duty was doing a very good job as we passed southbound freight trains and the westbound Indian Pacific on loops long enough to allow both trains to move slowly past each other without having to come to a complete stop.

This is the face of the future: an efficient single track main line operation supported with good communications, adequate loops and good traffic management. It is certainly a far cry from the agony on sections of bent rails between Melbourne and Sydney or between Newcastle and Brisbane, where until recently trains stopped, even when there was no oncoming traffic, for drivers to unlock a box and mechanically obtain clearance for the next section.

At the Crystal Brook junction, the line takes off for Broken Hill, Parkes and Sydney in one direction and Port Pirie, Port Augusta and beyond in the other. I pointed out the brook and the nearby new Australian Wheat Board silo complex with its own loop to my fellow passengers. The previous year the base fell out of one of the large new steel silos. The falling wheat acted as a plunger, sucking in and collapsing the roof of the silo. Luckily no one was killed. The Australian Wheat Board completed repairs just in time for the 2003 harvest.

The train gathered pace as it whipped along a double track section between Crystal Brook and Port Pirie, the only double track in the ARTC system. Helicopters were still pursuing the train, often making very low passes alongside to capture the superb footage that was beamed around the nation and the world over the next couple of days.

At Port Pirie we slowed to by-pass the city with its big refinery, wharf and break of gauge platform of yesteryear. It was here that passengers changed from the Commonwealth Railways standard gauge trains to the South Australian Irish broad gauge trains. In 2001, travelling on the special 'Tracks to Federation' Indian Pacific with the then governor general, Dr Peter Hollingworth, we pulled into the very large Port Pirie break of gauge platform for a truly spectacular community lunch. So as not to change the make up of the elongated train, it had to carefully reverse out of the station to pick up the main line and head north to Port Augusta for the long journey to Perth.

We had clear views of Spencer Gulf on the left and the mighty Flinders Ranges on the right as we headed up to the gap that constitutes Pichi Richi Pass and through to Quorn and ultimately Wilpena Pound. At Stirling North there was some confusion as to which level crossing we were to stop at to pick up the South Australian premier and other VIPs who had flown in by charter plane from Adelaide. The look on Premier Mike Rann's face as we surged past the crossing his driver had chosen could be compared to thunder clouds. The confusion was quickly sorted out and soon enough both the premier and the feisty mayor of Port Augusta, Joy Baluch, were on board.

Soon after, the Pichi Richi excursion train emerged on the parallel narrow gauge track for a special run from Quorn to Port Augusta. The magnificent steam engine pulled a number of vintage freight cars and a couple of old Ghan passenger carriages aided by an old Ghan Commonwealth Railways diesel engine. This glorious sight was topped off by a rust red wooden guard's van. As we looked out on this train in the shimmering heat of the late afternoon, I was very glad we were travelling in an air-conditioned crew car and not the ancient guard's van.

At the Port Augusta station I again had the pleasant job of acting as master of ceremonies to the huge crowd, many of whom had driven hundreds of miles to witness the occasion. The premier said a few words and, in conjunction with the mayor, FreightLink CEO Bruce McGowan and Barry Wakelin, federal member for Grey, he unveiled a commemorative plaque. In the large and thankfully air-conditioned waiting room Bruce McGowan joined the premier and Barry Wakelin in celebrating the project's prospects. Particular reference was made to connections between South Australia's iron triangle—Port Augusta, Port Pirie and Whyalla—and the Northern Territory; after all, 144 000 tonnes of steel rail had been shifted by special train from Whyalla through Port Augusta to Roe Creek near Alice Springs.

In welcoming everybody, the mayor had to get one thing off her mind. She told the gathering she was sick of hearing the master of ceremonies all day on the radio saying he wanted a 'cold stubbie' from the mayor on arrival at Port Augusta. She duly produced beer, gestured as if to hit me over the head but relented just in time to wish me well!

I was so dehydrated that I immediately proceeded to drink the beer, even before the mayor had finished her speech! I chided myself later, but this was all in keeping with the very happy spirit of the occasion. I then presented the president of the Pichi Richi railway, Phil Mellors, with a magnificent photo of a pre-1929 mixed passenger and freight train taken at Marree by the Reverend John Flynn well over 70 years before.

We were driven out to the freight yards, where the train had repositioned, and soon enough were thundering through the desert towards Woomera. The Flinders Ranges looked formidable in the sunset.

Near Pimba and the siding for Woomera lie a series of salt lakes. One lake in particular always catches my attention when I travel by train in the area. When sighted from a distance the sharp pimple of a hill in the middle of the lake is not unlike the silhouette of Mont St Michel, just off the north-west coast of France. (This famous abbey is about to have its own 6 kilometre branch line constructed to its sea wall. The line, which will carry both TGV and local services, is due to open in 2006.)

Radio broadcasts from the train continued throughout the night, including to BBC Radio. A live broadcast was also organised to go right across the nation to 57 ABC capital city and country radio stations. Normally anchored by Tony Delroy, the very popular *Nightline* program was tonight in the hands of Sarah McDonald, who was obviously as excited by the project as me.

It was around midnight and still people were coming from local station homesteads to isolated level crossings to take photographs and wave flags at 001 as it sped through the night to Tarcoola.

I was invited to go forward to the locomotive. I particularly wanted to inspect Tarcoola junction and chat with these highly professional drivers about their job. It had been a very long day, a very exhilarating day and a very exhausting day, so halfway through the conversation I promptly fell asleep to be woken by one of the drivers with the memorable words: 'You're sacked.'

'Fair enough,' I figured and just then Tarcoola loomed large with its various sidings for passing trains and shunting trains. There was also a small triangle for turning engines and a large triangle to allow trains from Perth and Kalgoorlie to turn directly to the north for Alice Springs and Darwin.

Despite the moment in history for tiny Tarcoola, this was the one place where everyone had gone to bed. There was not a soul to be seen. Perhaps the few hardy residents felt cheated. In April 1975 Gough Whitlam (then prime minister) and Charlie Jones (then trans-port minister) had come to Tarcoola to launch the construction of the direct Tarcoola to Alice Springs line. It was a grand ceremony with TV crews present, a plunger to trigger a detonator, a symbolic explosion and a plaque unveiling. There was even a locomotive naming ceremony. This time Tarcoola was not listed for any sort of ceremony, formal or informal, as it turned out.

In the distance I spotted the lights of the Pacific National crew resthouse. A lonely station building stood beside it, together with the de-licensed Tarcoola Hotel and not one, but two, telephone booths out the front all lit up.

One of the drivers had to step down and set the points to allow passage onto the Alice Springs line. These points are cunningly designed to reset after the train has passed. I took the opportunity of a crew change to go back to the crew car to try and get some sleep. Soon enough we were powering away on the track that had been opened in 1980 but for which a peppercorn fee had been paid to transfer it from ARTC to APT, as part of negotiations for the Darwin project.

I thought twice about waking up APT president Malcolm Kinnaird to inform him we were now on Malcolm's metals, deciding instead to have a quick shower and collapse into bed.

The four train drivers who took the first train from the Southern Ocean and Spencer Gulf to the Arafura Sea and Darwin's East Arm Harbour had years of experience. History will record them as being Mick Corey, Mick Fuller, Geoff Noble and Geoff Stansborough—the two Micks and the two Geoffs.

I listened carefully to their talk about 'mud holes' along the track, which could be easily seen in the locomotive searchlight. Over the previous few months, heavy rail track had pounded the concrete sleepers in sections where the ballast was loose. This had the effect of turning the ballast to powder and causing a dip as trains passed, even at speed. Between Pimba and Tarcoola one mud hole had caused the locomotive to lurch. The drivers reported this through to Port Augusta. The result was an immediate inspection in the middle of the night and the placement of an additional speed restriction of 40 kilometres per hour on this section of track pending repair.

I was greatly impressed by this swift response. Sadly many other rail systems in Australia can not match this alacrity.

In the morning I returned to the working lounge in the main crew car and found John Phillips, the man responsible for video recording the whole saga, doing a jig for joy. The four minute segment he had recorded out of Adelaide through to Port Augusta had been widely used the previous night on most network television news programs. In fact, SBS News used the entire segment.

I 'hit up' some further radio stations that had requested telephone calls and then bombarded one or two favourite programs, including Paul Dix's morning show on 2QN Deniliquin. All of the interviews were bright and breezy as people were keen to learn of the train's overnight progress.

One radio presenter repeatedly asked, 'Where exactly are you?' I had to make a swift guess. 'Very close to the South Australia–Northern Territory border.' Suddenly, in one of those lucky coincidences, the actual border sign came into view. We were entering the Northern Territory just after dawn. Darwin ABC was particularly excited with this and extended the interview for some eight minutes. Clearly Darwin was pumped up in expectation, more so than Alice Springs.

At the millionth sleeper marker on the Tarcoola to Port Augusta section, we stopped for a crew change and disembarked for a set of historic photos to be taken, including one of the first group of people to travel by train right through from Adelaide to Darwin. As is so often the case when the pressure is on, this group, who had in fact never ever met before, got on famously.

We had a schedule to keep so our stop was very short. Soon after, FreightLink service 001 crossed the mighty, but completely dry, Finke River. At one time, the river ran from central Australia all the way down to Spencer Gulf. Erosion means it now runs into the giant Lake Eyre system.

To the north the distant blue hue of the MacDonnell Ranges could be easily seen. As we readied for the next big ceremony, our mobile phone and satellite email dropped out. I joked that this was because of our proximity to Pine Gap, the joint Australian–United States military facility, it being a matter of public record that the base is able to intercept communications right around the world. With full communications restored, we saw a Qantas jet on final landing for the nearby Alice Springs airport. It was a kind of accidental fly past.

Kilometre by kilometre, we were now converging with the original narrow gauge track from Marree to Alice Springs, joining it just south of the Alice Springs showground. Near the end of the remnants of the narrow gauge, an old railway station has been converted into a museum housing a collection of railway memorabilia as well as original trucks and semi-trailers. The initiative of former speaker of the Northern Territory House of Assembly, Roger Vale, it struggles to survive, particularly in the hot season. Perhaps the new Ghan sweeping by to Darwin will help give the museum a much needed boost.

At last we slowed for the entry through the historic Heavitree Gap, discovered by the explorer John McDouall Stuart. Hundreds of people were waiting for us as we made our grand entry into the Alice Springs railway yards and station. Concern over the standard of the platform track meant that we were put through the main siding track. Engine drivers worldwide would be interested to know this resulted in the first train to Darwin being authorised to pass through a station entry signal that was red on red. I guessed we were the only train in town, but most drivers would be very uncomfortable even with authorisation to pass a signal saying 'stop and stop'.

We alighted and proceeded to the station building for the welcome ceremony. Security concerns meant that the crowd had been held back at a locked gate, however, it soon swarmed in and I caught up with many friends and wellwishers.

A bright new master of ceremonies (it was certainly time for a change), local comedian Fiona O'Laughlin, brought the crowd to order and commenced proceedings with the singing of the national anthem. Then, with the nearby locomotives brightly painted in northern and central Aboriginal motifs, Lhere Artepe elder, Betty Pearce warmly welcomed us on behalf of the Indigenous people of central Australia. In referring to Aboriginal Dreaming, she made the point that the new train was a much awaited giant steel caterpillar. While some of these welcome to country ceremonies in outback Australia have taken on a degree of political correctness, bordering on absurdity at times, on this occasion it was very appropriate, particularly given Central Land Council and Northern Land Council investment in the project.

Chief minister Clare Martin and South Australian premier Mike Rann spoke again, this time in reverse order reflecting that we had crossed the border. Clare had been true to her promise and brought a set of newspapers for those of us on board to read on the train.

Senator Nigel Scullion, in a shocking yellow shirt, spoke on behalf of the prime minister, while the final speaker, Bruce McGowan, reminded us of the importance of the freight services.

Camels in spectacular rig emerged from nowhere and made their way alongside the train to distribute bush tucker meal boxes, vanishing as quickly as they came. As chairman of the Australian Wine Foundation, a modest philanthropic organisation supporting Indigenous community projects in particular, I pointed out that we had recently approved seed funding to build camel drafting yards at the Docker River settlement. A strong business case had been developed to muster camels in the area and road them to the rail head at Alice Springs for both the domestic and export markets.

With local firefighters again on hand to give us a ceremonial farewell, we at last departed Alice Springs with the correct number of passengers on board and a train slightly reduced in length. The question returned in my mind, would we make the ascent up the Great Larapinta Grade without breaking down? The train not only swiftly moved into the climb, but continued to accelerate up the grade. Soon enough we swept smoothly through Cutting No. 5, over the famous Larapinta walking trail and into a set of brilliantly engineered curves. With the sun-drenched MacDonnell Ranges in the background, this section of the transcontinental presents some wonderful views and has become the favourite spot for aerial photographs.

We quickly stopped at the top of the grade to let some media off, and were again greeted by hundreds of people waiting in the fiercely hot conditions.

In between Alice Springs and Tennant Creek, some gremlins crept into the 240 volt on-board electricity system, affecting the crew cars and communication car but fortunately not the locomotive. It was almost as if the freight train proper was trying to rid itself of the blemish of the crew cars and the passenger observation car.

The electrician advised that the old observation car system was incompatible with the more modern crew cars and power unit, so was tripping the system out just as we were going into the hottest section of the journey. In the stifling heat on board, I decided to down tools, dip my head under the shower and lie down for a siesta. Being able to sleep in almost any situation, I woke an hour or two later in a boiling hot cabin but refreshed and ready to write up my diary.

While I was having my siesta, 001 had two long stops in the middle of nowhere, about an hour in total. The temperature climbed rapidly onboard, but fortunately the deep freeze and refrigerator retained just enough coolness to prevent the precious food and drink onboard from being written off. The offending observation car was isolated from the rest of the train and used its own generator.

Only an hour late, after some fast running to catch up time, we arrived at Tennant Creek mid evening to a warm welcome from the local Aboriginal people and the mayor, Paul Ruger, who runs a Tennant Creek road house. It was here that Bruce McGowan officially opened the FCL intermodal freight terminal. FCL had won the contract to operate both the Tennant Creek and Katherine terminals and already that afternoon an order had been received to shift four containers of bananas by road from Cairns to Tennant Creek then by rail to Perth.

It was by now around 10.00 pm and the crowd was excited. One teenage girl remarked to me, 'Geez mate, I've never seen so much talent in Tennant Creek … never has there been such an exciting gig here on a Friday night.' I should hasten to add that she wasn't looking at me at the time.

Soon enough we were on our way again, overnight to Katherine. Once again, locals had driven out from nearby pastoral stations during the night, waiting to wave through the first train to run to Darwin.

We woke on the final morning, Saturday 17 January, to a green landscape. The wet season had arrived in Katherine. It seemed that most of Katherine's 4000 residents had turned up for yet another warm welcome. I presented a bottle of Federation red wine to the mayor, Jim Forscutt, and to Bill Gibbons, head of FCL.

As we departed Katherine we crossed the mighty Katherine River, which had recently been in flood. The high standard of construction had ensured that heavy wet season rains and floods would not wipe out the railway to Darwin.

For the first time, remnants of the old Northern Australia Railway (NAR) narrow gauge track could be clearly seen, including some of the disused bridges with girders still intact. At Adelaide River, where there is a magnificent NAR heritage precinct, someone had kindly written a sign in very large letters simply saying, 'Welcome Tim'. This was almost enough to make me think about going back into politics. On snap reflection, I quickly ruled this out.

Buried in the jungle just over the Adelaide River is a labyrinth of narrow gauge railway loops and sidings. Known as the Snake Creek munitions storage area, this railway system was used intensively during World War II. Fortunately all the explosives have been removed and destroyed as local volunteers are now trying to reinstate it as a tourist railway. From time to time I have tried to assist them. Given its proximity to Darwin, there is every chance that the project will be a success.

As we were now quite close to Darwin, the crowds on both sides of the track continued to grow. Unfortunately, many missed out on seeing this first train to Darwin as we were ahead of schedule to allow plenty of time to pick up the prime minister in Darwin.

By now I had been asked to do hourly live to air broadcasts to ABC radio in Darwin, particularly to urge people to stand well clear of the track as the train's momentum made it very difficult to stop quickly. What I should have also done was give the exact location of the train so people would know when it would be passing by.

The local rag, the *NT News*, made a big issue of the fact that some locals missed the opportunity to see 001, thus diminishing the very positive impact this transcontinental railway will have on the Territory. Over the years the *NT News* has sometimes been dubbed the 'Territory terrible' tabloid.

On board we had a last supper, a light lunch of salad and rolls.

With brilliant timing, Malcolm Kinnaird produced a magnificent bottle of chardonnay. Grand occasions should be celebrated properly.

I missed seeing my friend Mick Dennigan, of Mick's Whips, at the level crossing leading to his eco-lodge and one of the largest whip factories in the world. Things were getting very busy as we curved around the edge of the Arafura Sea and crossed the last of 97 bridges, the Elizabeth River bridge. Located on a saltwater estuary just short of Palmerston, this is the longest bridge on the railway.

Looking north, the modest skyscrapers of the Darwin CBD were clearly visible. Somewhere in between stood the Berrimah terminal, the Great Southern Railway Darwin station and the East Arm wharf complex. Signs of welcome had been erected and landscape improvements undertaken at the nearby city of Palmerston. Unfortunately, this was not enough to encourage the Northern Territory government to place the passenger railway station there as had been requested by the mayor, Annette Burke.

The crowd continued to grow on either side of the track until we reached the last short section of tropical jungle. We then entered the Berrimah freight yard and Darwin station complex for a quick shunt and to pick up the prime minister, John Howard, and his wife Janette.

A crowd of well over 5000 people, indeed some estimated it at 10000, had gathered on the East Arm wharf as the first freight service slipped around the curve, coming to a halt ten metres short of the dais. We could now clearly see Darwin CBD just a few kilometres over the water, and this led to a stunning front page photo in the Melbourne *Sunday Age* showing the first train, the glistening water of East Arm wharf and Darwin in the background.

RAAF jets flew overhead, the band played, the crowd roared, parachutists landed and balloons went up—it was brilliantly organised mayhem! Despite the heat there was great excitement as the crowd listened to speeches from the prime minister, the president of Halliburton, the South Australian premier and the Northern Territory chief minister. I was invited to call for three big cheers for the world's newest and smoothest transcontinental.

I also took the opportunity to hand out copies of *Railway Digest*, noting that these magazines could now be termed historic as they were the first to travel by rail from Adelaide to Darwin. In my baggage I still had some intact bottles of Federation red wine, the first ever to travel by rail between Adelaide and Darwin. I recognised that I was perhaps overdoing the 'first ever' aspect of the trip. Nevertheless, the mood was so upbeat it was easy to get away with almost anything! (The red wine was subsequently sold at a charity auction down south for a suitably generous bid.)

I sat in the front row with Barry Coulter, the long-serving Northern Territory minister for railways, who had put enormous energy into getting the project started. He very much appreciated the recognition he received from a number of speakers.

Sadly, one important group was ignored during the speeches—the surveyors, including Des Smith, who led the survey project from its commencement in 1980. Over the years he was joined by many fellow surveyors, including Garry Nairn, Federal Member for Eden Monaro. Their efforts resulted in 60 kilometres of track distance being saved between Alice Springs and Darwin compared to the highway route, which in turn provided a financial saving of over $70 million. Their precise work had taken the railway route east of the Stuart Highway on the section between Alice Springs and Tennant Creek and west of the Stuart Highway between Tennant Creek and Katherine.

The reception at the wharf after the formalities were over was a dry affair. The no alcohol decision had been taken after some members of the community complained that there would be grog for some but not for all. You have to know the Northern Territory to understand how seriously they take their grog. The problem was solved by the Northern Territory government putting everyone on the same footing by supplying only soft drinks and water. One journalist wrote later that had the Country Liberal Party still been in power in the Northern Territory, it would have been a case of grog for all and plenty of it!

In due course, it was a mini van trip into town for a quick swim and a borrowed bowtie before setting off to dinner at Darwin's magnificent new Parliament House. It was a memorable dinner and this time we had wine to toast 001's arrival in Darwin. I spoke to the prime minister about the long process of approval and we recalled the phone call between him, the treasurer Peter Costello and myself many years before that set the project in train.

Some of the gathering went on to a local nightclub, but I took Malcolm Kinnaird back to his hotel by car. I had a 5.45 am departure and it was already past midnight. Alas, I thought, I must be getting old.

The first new piece of major transport infrastructure in decades had at last been opened. It had certainly been a privilege to have been involved and to travel on that first freight train. Many people had a right to be very proud.

As I later reviewed some of the photos and television coverage I noted a small change had been made at Alice Springs. The two brightly painted locomotives had been swapped around so the locomotive bearing the central Australia motif, the Purna, led the train into Alice Springs while the locomotive into Darwin, the Kurra Kurraka, was decorated in the Aboriginal motif of the Top End. The appropriateness of this swap became even more obvious when I learnt that *Purna* is an Aboriginal word meaning something used to carry things, and *Kurra Kurraka* means storm bird. Clearly nothing had been left to chance.

On the Sunday, the day after the first train arrived in Darwin from Adelaide, there were enough people around, despite the hangovers, to received 6AD1. This second freight train, with 99 containers on board, was longer and heavier than the first, having a gross trailing load just two tonnes short of 3000 tonnes. Messages of congratulations streamed in from all over the world, from Junee in Australia's Riverina to Cannes in the Riviera, expressing delight at the success of the railway.

As I write, 50 freight trains have gone through in both directions, although some speed restrictions have been applied to ease container vibrations pending further harmonisation of rail wheel and rail head profiles. Shipments of containers have been loaded from rail to ship for Asia and domestic freight has expanded in both directions. Even the army has used the freight service, shifting large equipment to exercises in the Northern Territory in March 2004.

The focus at both ends now turned towards the next big event— the first trip of the legendary Ghan from Adelaide to Darwin.

CHAPTER FIFTEEN

THE FIRST GHAN TO DARWIN

What on earth would make the running of the first Ghan to Darwin truly enjoyable, exciting and memorable? What would make it a headline-grabbing, history-making transport event? Would the public respond positively, given the disdain expressed in certain quarters of the media? These were reasonable questions to ask two weeks after the first freight train from Adelaide to Darwin completed its trip and on the day The Ghan was to begin its first through service to Darwin.

As it turned out, Great Southern Railway (GSR) and, to a lesser extent, the three governments directly involved need not have been overly concerned. For a range of reasons, the first Ghan from St Vincent Gulf and Adelaide to Beagle Gulf, the Arafura Sea and Darwin hit the right nerve with the Australian public.

So many Australians had either travelled on the old Ghan or learnt about its colourful history in school. The stop start fortnight-long trips through the flooded outback became part of national folklore. It has also been a long time since a new railway, let alone a trans-continental railway, has been built in Australia. In fact, it could probably be said this was the first transcontinental to be built anywhere in the world in the last 80 years.

Despite the cynical local media, many people had their interest awakened by that first freight train and the vivid television coverage that accompanied it. News of the first Ghan to Darwin therefore resonated around the world. BBC-TV and CNN covered the event. It even reached the tiny railwayless kingdom of Bhutan where the Bhutan Broadcasting Corporation (the other BBC) picked up the story. This was a grand media event that augured well for the future of one of the world's great railway journeys.

Judy and I arrived at Adelaide's Keswick terminal on Sunday 1 February 2004 to find the inaugural Ghan to Darwin glistening in the morning sunshine between the odd shower of rain. The night before we had attended a magnificent state dinner hosted by GSR and premier Mike Rann. Camels in the courtyard of the sandstone Adelaide railway station set the scene as the railway was toasted, and roasted, well into the night.

We were quickly ushered through the check-in to find our carriage and berth on the 1.1 kilometre long train. For loading purposes the train had been divided into three sections, each with its own platform. After the official ceremony, it was then assembled into one very long train, breaking all southern hemisphere passenger train records. Guest services and marketing director, Anthony Kirchner, the 'Person Friday', master of ceremonies and overall co-ordinator, was doing a fabulous job to ensure a departure on time.

Just before boarding Judy and I ran into former prime minister Gough Whitlam and his wife Margaret. They were in the Prince of Wales car, a magnificent old wooden carriage with thick carpets, comfortable lounge chairs and private apartments. This carriage was beautifully restored, although the polished wood did creak from time to time as the train accelerated or braked.

Gough boldly asked us where the kids were. Those marrying later in life always pushed their kids forward as a badge of honour, he suggested. Without intending or giving offence, he looked directly at me and said, as only Gough can, this was a well-recognised phenomenon.

The kids out of the way, we talked about gauge and rail co-ordination problems in Australia, agreeing that the 'Feds' should have taken over the non-metropolitan railway systems, if not between the wars, then in the early 1970s. In one sense this is happening now with the agreement between ARTC, the federal rail network corporation, and the Rail Infrastructure Corporation, New South Wales' rail track organisation.

With its gleaming brass fittings and rich green painted casing, the magnificently preserved little steam engine 'the Sandfly' was bolted down on the main platform, which was just as well as it once operated on the old Northern Australia Railway out of Darwin, so really belonged to the Northern Territory. I was informed by ex-GSR head Stephen Bradford that there had been many tussels over ownership of this historic and romantic engine. While not as passionately fought over as the return of the Parthenon Marbles, one of Gough's great causes, debate was vigorous enough.

Our berth wasn't as grand as Gough and Margaret's, but it was comfortable enough and easy to relax in. Soon after we settled, The Ghan began rolling forward to break through a special banner, letting off streamers and fireworks. The long journey north had begun.

There was a little bit of 'rock and rolling', particularly when we crossed over the Port Dock Irish broad gauge double track, but after passing the freight yards we accelerated on the main line north. (It has to be said, the ARTC maintained standard gauge to Port Augusta and beyond is smoother than any standard gauge in New South Wales.)

As is always the case on a luxury passenger train, passengers from all walks of life soon linked up. Many of us gathered in one of the large and comfortable lounge cars to celebrate the departure and introduce and be introduced to one another. Our comfortable tranquility was soon given a bit of a jolt with a bizarre salute to the first Ghan. Near Nantawarra, not far to the north of Adelaide, several women stood along the track and lifted their blouses to reveal all! This was somewhat more polite than the bare bottom salute that later greeted us in the Territory.

Like brightly coloured gadflies, helicopters buzzed the train at extraordinarily low levels. I prayed they were communicating with one another and were in no danger of colliding.

Our call to lunch was delivered in great style, and in a wonderfully rich and thick Dutch accent, by chief conductor and chief steward, Jos Engelaar. The dignified but colourful Jos made the most of the occasion. We were joined for the sumptuous lunch by the South Australian leader of the opposition, Rob Kerin. As the member for the district we were travelling through, he happily pointed out many local features, including his own small family business on the outskirts of Crystal Brook. I recounted how, at the nearby Riverton railway station, Australia's first political assassination took place when, in 1921, Percy Brookfield, the member for the NSW state seat of Sturt, was shot trying to disarm a gunman. As I looked out the window, I realised how lucky I was to be on board, especially in the knowledge that there were no mad gunmen on the train.

There was a certain joy in seeing over a kilometre of train ahead of you and behind you no matter where you were seated. The vista from the 'steel crocodile', as this train had been nicknamed, was far better than anything that could be captured on video. Seeing the two red-coloured Ghan locomotives in the lead and two motor rail carriages in the rear conferred a comfort that simply can never be matched by air or sea travel.

We passed four freight trains between Adelaide and Port Augusta, including one on the double-tracked section between Crystal Brook and Port Pirie. None of the passing trains had to stop, which says a lot about the efficiency of the scheduling. On a Sunday afternoon on the southern half of the Sydney–Melbourne main line you would be lucky to see just one freight train and, if you did, this would more than likely have been a seasonal bulk wheat train. The truth is Sydney–Melbourne rail freight is staggering while Adelaide–Perth is performing very well.

It was late afternoon when we came through Stirling North to cross over the Leigh Creek branch line and find, once again, the Pichi

Richi locomotive steaming alongside. Sadly not everybody on The Ghan had the chance to see the Pichi Richi in full motion as there was no radio communication between the steam locomotive and The Ghan locomotive. Those of us lucky enough to catch a glance saw a recreation of the old narrow gauge Ghan, which included some flat top railway wagons carrying vintage cars. With particular attention to detail, these magnificent cars were tied down with thick rope that had been tightened by a classic twitch using a stick that was long enough to lock itself on to the wagon floor. This was a wonderful effort by a bunch of very dedicated volunteers who have rebuilt the narrow gauge track between Quorn and Port Augusta through Stirling North.

The Ghan glided into Port Augusta's main platform, while the packed out Pichi Richi train terminated on the adjoining narrow gauge platform.

The entire train disembarked to enjoy the carnival atmosphere at the redeveloped foreshore park which was to be opened by Premier Mike Rann. Port Augusta had once been a busy port, the closest not only central Australia but also to the productive channel country of south- west Queensland. Years ago clipper ships sailed north from Port Augusta to Liverpool in the United Kingdom carrying wool, while on the southbound journey they carried essential supplies, including Scotch whisky and rum.

Joy Baluch, Port Augusta's long-serving and at times irreverent mayor, was presented with a certificate celebrating the inaugural Ghan to Darwin. Her response was immediate: 'Thanks, but where's my ticket?' Her fellow townspeople enjoyed this enormously. Alas, she remained ticketless.

The crowd of several thousand was very good humoured and friendly, and its size a little surprising. Port Augusta had seen trains for over 125 years and The Ghan in its various manifestations for most of the last 75 years. However, the crowd recognised this was a special, history-making trip. It was also a pleasant Sunday afternoon, and I guess there is not all that much else to do in Port Augusta late on a summer weekend.

As we walked back to the station I thought about going for a swim in the Spencer Gulf in a small town pool fenced off by mesh to keep the sharks away. I had my togs in hand, but one look from my wife told me it probably wouldn't be such a wise idea.

Just before departure, I was presented with a magnificent mounting of a section of the old narrow gauge rail by the Pichi Richi president Phil Mellors. As a patron of the railway, I was genuinely touched by this thoughtful gesture.

Pre-dinner drinks hosted by Chris Hyman, the chairman of Serco, owner of Great Southern Railway, were scheduled in the Hans Heysen car (named after the great Australian landscape artist who lived in the Adelaide Hills and spent much of his lifetime capturing the beauty of the nearby Flinders Ranges). The company, which operates many light rail services in the northern hemisphere and is a multi-billion dollar enterprise, employs just 45 people in its London headquarters.

I learnt later that Chris had been in the World Trade Center on the morning of September 11 and had had a very narrow escape. It is clear that, having survived the experience and the very difficult days that followed, Chris was determined to make every moment of his life count. He has plenty of drive, literally, as he is also a racing car driver.

Judy and I enjoyed the late dinner sitting with Denis and Annette Burke. Denis had been the Country-Liberal Party chief minister of the Northern Territory at the time the project commenced. He was both happy and sad to see it come to fruition under someone else's watch. (Denis lost the 2001 election to Clare Martin and the ALP.) In any event, Annette continues to carry the family's political torch as the popular mayor of Darwin's neighbouring city, Palmerston. Annette was banking on The Ghan being right on time into Darwin so she could make it to Tuesday night's council meeting.

The Ghan roared past the lights of the township of Woomera just to the north of Pimba Siding, where more people had gathered to cheer the train through. We were running ahead of schedule, so the drivers notched the throttle back a little and we had a very smooth and steady journey into the night, taking the gradual turn at Tarcoola junction with ease.

The sunrise was spectacular as The Ghan approached the South Australia–Northern Territory border. A signpost on the eastern side of the track marked the border but there was nothing on the western side. I made the suggestion to Mike Rann and Clare Martin that a large commemorative sculpture be erected to celebrate Australia's newest transcontinental railway. 'Not a bad idea,' remarked the premier, 'particularly as The Ghan will cross the border in both directions in daylight.'

As we gathered for breakfast the still dry mighty Finke River came into view. I looked further east towards the horizon, to see the silent sentinel known as Chambers Pillar. With the early morning sun rising almost directly behind it, the rock pillar looked sinister and very imposing.

Judy and I shared a hearty breakfast with Simon and Carole Crean, who were most relaxed in the aftermath of Simon's loss of the leadership of the federal Labor Party. We swapped anecdotes on the rigours of political life, especially the impact it has on kids. Then, in what seemed like a blink of an eye, we were on the outskirts of Alice Springs.

We rolled slowly through Heavitree Gap (this time the signals were green on green) into a sharp curve to stop at an empty platform. For security reasons the public was being held behind a locked gate until ten minutes after The Ghan arrived. We were then quickly ushered onto large coaches for the drive into town for a lunch at the Alice Springs Convention Centre.

Over the decades I have attended all sorts of functions; some have been very creative and a pleasure to be at, others were completely hopeless. The great idea that lifted this lunch into the special category was that a student and a parent from every school in Alice Springs had been selected to sit at each table, from the top table right down. The children were wide eyed but not a bit overwhelmed by the dignitaries. They were great company.

We were entertained by a live presentation of a School of the Air lesson. The several hundred people present heard kids from isolated stations all over central Australia talk with their teacher about the big event of the day.

Before we reboarded the train, an excited Shannon Kilgarrif, granddaughter of the former senator, told the gathering how her family had woken at dawn to drive 90 kilometres from Eldunda Station to Kulgera Siding, just north of the South Australia–Northern Territory border, to wave to The Ghan as it swept by. The excitement of this transcontinental railway had not waned in the two weeks since the first freight train passed through.

The Ghan wasted no time in accelerating up the Great Larapinta Grade out of Alice Springs. With the mighty MacDonnell Ranges in the background, professional and amateur photographers had worked out that this was the best location to get some truly spectacular photos of The Ghan on the new track.

Unfortunately the view from on board was rather more limited. Someone suggested that Great Southern Rail invest in a double-decker observation car. Certainly, it should examine the second-hand railway carriage market particularly in the United States, where Amtrack continues to build such cars.

Just north of Alice Springs, we experienced the one blemish in the performance of our berth. The toilet decided to malfunction somewhere near the Devil's Marbles, permeating a particularly fulsome odour through the carriage. This slight hiccup was resolved by a sustained attack with pressurised deodorant cans operated by the ever-flexible and hard-working train crew.

We settled into the train routine all too easily. There were more cocktail parties, an ebb and flow of people along the carriages and lots of chat. Judy and I joined Nick and Kerry Minchin for dinner. Nick had previously been industry minister and was now federal minister for finance. Over the years he and I had been taunted with the jibe that in every economic dry there is at least one wet spot; in our case it was the railway. Mind you, I maintain I was always a dry with qualifications.

As it was necessary to complete both dinner sittings in time for our arrival in Tennant Creek, the staff had to work even harder than usual. They managed brilliantly in the confined space, maintaining their smiling faces as always.

At Tennant Creek half the town again turned out. Under the bright spotlights, a local Aboriginal dance group performed a welcome to country ceremony, which I gather had been a surprise addition to the program.

Judy and I spent much of our last night on this inaugural Ghan listening to one of Australia's leading country performers, James Blundell, sing some old favourites, including 'American Pie'. One wag remarked this was a very appropriate song as the Americans owned a large chunk of the project through Asia Pacific Transport.

It was well after 1.00 am when James pleaded the need to go to bed. Few people had trouble sleeping on the second night as we were all exhausted and the smooth ride provided the gentlest rocking.

At dawn The Ghan reached the southern outskirts of Katherine. There had been a great deal of rain so the landscape was even greener than it had been a fortnight earlier and stood in deep contrast to the inland desert and the brown plains of the south. The mayor, Jim Forscutt, extended a warm welcome, only to be upstaged by one of the Aboriginal elders who quipped: 'We used to move by foot, then by Toyota, but now by glorious train.'

James Blundell launched into his special song about The Ghan, the crowd taking up the chorus with gusto:

> Out of South Australia to the territory
> Travelling to Darwin, Feeling free
> There is no other place I would rather be
> Than on The Ghan.
> Rattle through The Alice, back into South Australia
> With the morning sun we hit Adelaide
> What a way to spend a couple of days
> On the mighty Ghan.

Not to be outdone by the visitor the local choir, the Kantaballey Choir, gave a bright, melodic rendition of 'This Train is Bound for Glory'. It certainly is.

During the ceremony federal Minister for Tourism Joe Hockey made a very brave public confession. He owned up to having bet me that the railway to Darwin would never ever be built. If he lost, he would run naked around Parliament House at an agreed time. The gathering was mightily relieved when Joe told them I had relieved him of the bet the night before. South Australian governor, Margery Jackson Nelson, immediately offered an alternative payout: 'Well Joe, you could run the length of the train . . .'. This he declined to roars of laughter.

There was no doubt the crowd at Katherine was bigger for The Ghan than it had been for the freight train, but at Tennant Creek it was the other way around. (For many locals, these two trains were the first they had ever seen.) Like so many communities in outback Australia, Tennant Creek and Katherine have suffered a recent decline that will now hopefully be a thing of the past. The new railway is seen as an economic panacea, with the two intermodal freight hubs operated by FCL being a key to the future.

We headed off on the final leg of the trip through Pine Creek and Adelaide River, where we made an unscheduled stop. During our last lunch on board, we looked out across lagoons formed by wet season flooding and to the nearby Stuart Highway. A convoy of cars had formed trying to pace the train. At some stage just before the railway peeled off to the west of the highway, we were regaled by 60 or so bare bottoms. Fortunately, I missed seeing this very different salute to The Ghan.

The Elizabeth River bridge soon emerged from the mangroves and The Ghan slowly rolled into Berrimah yards for a 'break the banner' ceremony and on to the platform.

During the small ceremony at Darwin station, I met up with Sue Wallace, a journalist from Albury's *Border Mail*. Sue and I have known one another for many years. She had travelled to Darwin that day to see The Ghan arrive and had the good fortune of being invited onboard for the return journey to Adelaide.

Somehow Judy and I became separated and only caught up with one another at our hotel in Darwin as we prepared for the gala dinner on the wharf that night. I was invited to propose the toast to the transcontinental and I was also able to make reference to a 90-year-old man who had paid his way from Adelaide to Darwin, and to correct the record that Gough Whitlam was the oldest person on board.

No matter what our circumstances, no matter our ages, every one of us who travelled on that inaugural Ghan had a truly memorable experience that will last forever.

In all the excitement I had forgotten about some precious cargo in my baggage. On unpacking at home, and worried that I'd have rum marinated baggage, I found several bottles of intact Bundaberg Rum I had been carrying on behalf of the Bundaberg Railway Historical Society. I sent these, the first bottles of Bundaberg Rum to travel from Adelaide to Darwin by rail, to the historical society as mementos of a fabulous trip.

The Ghan had arrived in Darwin. In doing so, it had touched a nerve with thousands of people and reminded us all of how dynamic rail can be. Given the recent failures of the Eastern and Orient Great South Pacific Express, running between Cairns and Brisbane, will The Ghan succeed? I think this train is bound for glory for many reasons.

First, The Ghan's carriages are over half a metre wider than those on the Great Southern Express, due to the generous loading gauge. In Queensland the Anglo Cape narrow gauge resulted in luxurious but cramped compartments and corridors. The Ghan is as spacious as any long-distance train in the world. The shower cubicles are generous, although the fold-down toilets can be a challenge. (They were given the nickname 'the Beast' by many of the women on board!) By the end of 2005, all of the sewage will be collected off the train at service points with nothing spilling onto the railway tracks, a kindly gesture to the track inspectors and fettlers.

Second, for half of its journey The Ghan runs on new, very smooth, well designed and well laid track over terrain that is mostly completely level, a rail engineer's dream. The Queensland northern main line, on the other hand, has been upgraded, but it still has many sharp curves and difficult terrain to contend with.

Third, over the decades The Ghan has been constantly upgraded, in terms not only of carriage comfort, but also in terms of marketing focus. Improved flight frequency and cheap air fares have caused many well-known passenger trains to be axed around the world, for example, the Twentieth Century Limited between New York and Chicago and the Mistral from Paris to the south of France. In Australia, the massive switch to airline travel wiped out the Spirit of Progress and the Southern Aurora. Sydney and Melbourne is now one of the biggest aviation pairs in the world with millions of people travelling between these two cities annually. Long-distance train services that have survived this onslaught have done so by marketing their trips as a travel experience. The Ghan to Darwin is a new tourist product, but not a new train.

The Ghan does not have exclusive rights to the Adelaide to Darwin rail track. Anyone can start up a train and run it to Darwin, so long as they pay FreightLink for access rights. George Milaras, who helped develop the Shongololo service in Africa, is investigating a similar form of rail cruising in Australia with his Ozback Explorer. He is planning trips that would be at least a week long in superbly fitted-out carriages. The train would carry buses that could be used for local excursions and the schedules would be geared to the seasons. During central Australia's wildflower season, for example, a sixteen day trip would take passengers from Sydney to Darwin via Canberra and Melbourne with many stops along the way.

Australia now has a transcontinental of such a high engineering standard that it will be an example of how to build conventional standard gauge rail in this century. Its very existence will force the upgrading of the bent tracks between Melbourne, Sydney and Brisbane. This could not happen soon enough.

In 1913 the Reverend John Flynn wrote:

> Central Australia is the core of a big whole, and it needs to be bored through, bored through with a railway. Then we can begin to talk about 'Our Country', rather than our scraps of country. It is easier to connect with Darwin as to build from London to Cairo. The line at present runs by Melbourne and Adelaide to Oodnadatta, more than half way. A little over a thousand miles will connect that distant place with Pine Creek, which is already joined by rail to Darwin. But some of this line is light and narrow and must be made wider and heavier for transcontinental traffic.

With the completion of the Adelaide to Darwin transcontinental railway, Flynn of the Inland can now rest easy in his grave at Alice Springs but his spirit of the outback is alive and well.

PART FOUR

THE FUTURE

3801

3801

CHAPTER SIXTEEN
A RAIL RENAISSANCE

The dynamic of rail is best summarised by the statement that a steel wheel on a steel rail has one seventh of the friction of a rubberised wheel on a bitumen surface. Rail is the way of the future. Gone with the smoke and soot of steam engines are the cabooses and guard vans, the single car railmotors and the quaint mixed passenger and freight trains.

We now have full length double-stacked container trains, double-decker high-speed passenger trains such as France's TGVs and Japan's Shinkansen and incredibly smart 'customer information systems' such as the cricket pitch length display board at London's Euston station. These systems can independently read point settings to reach a conclusion on a train's progress, often factoring in speed restrictions, to automatically update arrival and departure boards.

Change is the one constant that can be written into the future of rail: change in design, change in engineering, change in ownership structures and change in industrial relations. All of these have helped greatly to improve rail service and performance and thus its competitiveness.

Still, there are many questions to ask. Will there be any more new transcontinental railways? While Cairo to Cape Town remains very unlikely, it is not outside the realms of possibility that the Buenos

Aires to Santiago and Valparaiso will be built one day. And what about underground networks? Big cities around the world will have to build extra lines and, indeed, new underground systems as road congestion becomes an insurmountable problem. Will there be new TGV-type networks in the United States? Maybe, but there is a greater chance for major city pairs, such as Orlando to Tampa, to be linked properly, a project being pushed by Virgin Air's Richard Branson for completion by 2009. And what about changes to freight transport? Intermodal networks using rail, road and air will provide even greater economic advantages in the future and greater flexibility in freight movements.

For all of this to happen, the right kind of ownership and operational policies will need to apply. And while it will not be a case of one shoe fitting all, there will be some elements common to all realms.

In Europe, for example, government-owned railways will compete directly with privately owned railways. In some European countries the actual rail tracks will remain government owned while the train services will be operated privately. The key to success will be to ensure that services are able to operate across the different railway systems without disruption. This is particularly important at national borders.

It is for this reason France and Italy are looking at the ultimate rail tunnel, a 52 kilometre long super tunnel to be dug deep down below the original Mount Cenis mountain railway. With a generous loading gauge for both freight and high-speed passenger services, it will carry rail traffic from France to Italy and beyond. Even the antagonists Spain and Morocco have agreed to build a 39 kilometre double track rail tunnel under the Straits of Gibraltar, with a forecast opening in 2015.

Trans European driver training and testing is essential. Before long one driver will take a train all the way through from Warsaw to London, for example, in one shift. Swapping drivers at borders is both expensive and time consuming, especially as high-speed mail and passenger trains will travel this distance in less than ten hours within the next decade or two.

As well as harmonising all railway signal systems, both externally and in cabin, a decision will need to be made on a common language for all drivers, something decreed by the European Commission. In international aviation English is the universal language, although many pilots will imitate an Italian or German accent if they think it will get them further up the queue at Rome or Frankfurt airports. Rail in Europe has not reached this stage, but whenever there is a delay or an emergency, the matter of driver language becomes critical.

While Europe has invested heavily in rail, this cannot be said for much of the rest of the world. Adequate and efficient capital expenditure is essential for rail to survive and thrive. The bandaid approach to rail infrastructure will no longer work.

Take Sydney and Melbourne, Australia's two largest cities and largest manufacturing and general freight hubs. Both state and federal governments have invested heavily in upgrading the Hume Highway between the two cities with the intention that it become a six lane dual carriageway. But what are the environmental costs of a six lane highway compared to upgrading the standard gauge double rail track? To my way of thinking, the answer is pretty obvious: investment in rail is an investment in the environmental health of the nation.

And what about re-opening consideration of a high-speed train between Sydney, Canberra and Melbourne? The master plan for Sydney's Mascot airport provides for a tripling of passengers and a doubling of flights over the next 20 years. As pressure builds to expand the airport (a second Sydney airport remaining as unlikely as ever), the need for a TGV-type fast rail service becomes all the more obvious. Some will say pigs might fly first, but it needs to be remembered that not so long ago there was deep scepticism that the Adelaide to Darwin railway or a Eurotunnel would ever be built.

The powerful road lobby must be challenged and encouraged to support road and rail solutions. Billions of dollars are invested on roads annually in Australia, yet railways which are recognised as being economically efficient and environmentally friendly receive barely a fraction of this investment. National priorities must change.[1]

As important as capital investment is, competition is also essential. History has shown very starkly that complete monopolies ultimately become inefficient. Without the dynamics conferred by competition, costs and overheads go up rapidly, bureaucracy grows and passengers and customers can end up running a poor third to the needs of management and workers. Competition can take place between rail operators as well as between other modes of transport. There is also a need for competition between above-rail and below-rail operations.

Competition below rail can simply occur by outsourcing track maintenance through competitive tendering and harnessing the flexibility and energy of experienced private contractors. There must, of course, be provision to monitor very closely the performance of those contractors.

Above-rail competition continues to evolve, especially as deregulation in some of the big railway realms is less than ten years old. Other realms, such as India and Russia, have yet to commence the process. In the United States rail freight competition is ruthless, driving significant innovation and efficiencies. This competition was one of the factors behind Southern Pacific developing double-stack freight train operations in 1977. It is also why the United States is well ahead of Europe in the amount of freight going by rail.

For both freight and passenger services intermodal connections will be the key to the future, no matter what the realm. This has become so obvious that today there is barely a major international airport without a connecting rail service. In the case of Charles de Gaulle Airport in Paris the French have provided a coach from the terminal to the Central Airport railway station. This modern station provides not only a Resaux Expresse Regional service to downtown Paris but also platforms for direct TGV services to Calais, Bordeaux

1. In Australia the new Auslink policy developed by deputy prime minister John Anderson evaluates both rail and road for transport solutions.

and Lyons. Even better are airport terminals such as Frankfurt and Zurich with underground railway platforms within easy walking distance.

In Australia, airport services have a long way to go. Melbourne and Adelaide need intermodal underground rail stations at their airports. Sydney does have an airport link, developed as a public–private partnership. Unfortunately, it runs on a separate ticket system and fare structure and is thus not fully integrated into the Sydney service. For future intermodal services, it may be necessary to create special infrastructure bonds to help raise the necessary funds so that future generations, who will benefit from new super subways, will make a contribution to the cost of construction.

The Europeans, particularly in Belgium, have shown how freight intermodal can be perfected by building freight terminals for road and rail ahead of demand. At Delta 3 near Brussels, containers can be lifted directly from canal barges onto road trucks or rail wagons. France's mighty SNCF is examining a new roll on and roll off truck on rail system, known as Modalohr, to help move freight through the alps. Environmental concerns about choking diesel fumes in the narrow valleys leading up to the Mont Blanc tunnel has forced this initiative. The male population in this area is reported to be suffering increased levels of impotency and sterility as a consequence of the carbon monoxide in the air. Austria has also forced trucks onto rail to ease environmental burdens.

In Texas, the giant Texas Alliance hub sits on part of a ranch owned until a few years ago by Ross Perrot. In less than a decade, this open plain, cattle grazing country has been developed into warehouses and assembly factories with attached airport, road tarmac and rail sidings.

Australia is gradually improving its intermodal freight options, with Adelaide and Perth being further ahead of the game than the other capital cities. The small regional cities of Parkes and Wodonga, both strategically located in the Brisbane–Sydney and Melbourne– Adelaide quadrangle, have taken the initiative not shown by some capital cities in developing freight hubs. FCL is well established in

Parkes (which still has plans to develop an international freight airport), while the concrete pour to start the logistic hub at Wodonga is set for early 2005.

Above all else, the direct standard gauge rail corridor between Melbourne and Brisbane needs to be redeveloped principally for double-stacked container freight. The syndicate Great Australian Trunk Rail system is working on plans and seeking backers to build the missing link. Originally proposed by Everald Compton, plans have been frustrated by bureaucratic inertia.

Without seamless intermodal capability, container rail freight is dead, even on the Panama transcontinental. Norfolk Southern, who operate this railway, has invested heavily in the latest NCR Teradata computer system to ensure its rail operation maintains its ascendancy over Panama shipping. This system, which is also used by Qantas and helped it recover very quickly after the transport downturn post September 11, can read bookings and sales in real time and adjust shifts accordingly. Freight is forever changing so systems such as Teradata can boost productivity and eliminate waste.

However, no matter how technologically advanced freight operations are, if rail management remains inflexible and bureaucratically constrained, rail services are doomed. The giant bureaucracies of British Rail and the Indian railways, for example, need efficient management structures from top to bottom, without too many layers in between, suppported by strong leadership. They also need to find a way to encourage effective communication between management, the workforce, unions and passengers and customers and stop internal bickering. The simple fact is that decades ago feather bedding, duplication and waste could be tolerated. This is no longer the case. Everybody from the general public to the shrill media and demanding politicians and bankers are looking for efficient rail services and operations.

Sadly, however, in this search for efficiency and financial viability rail safety and security have been compromised, at times with disastrous consequences as seen with the October 2002 rail crash at Hatfield in the United Kingdom. Seven lives were lost and over 200 people injured when a high-speed train was derailed as a result of broken track. A charge of 'gross negligence manslaughter' was brought against the companies responsible for the maintenance and operation of the line. In Sydney, a sufficient number of drivers jammed the deadman's handle to a dangerous over-ride position to leave indentation marks. This was only discovered after a driver suffered a heart attack, derailing his train. Seven people died in the accident. It is therefore vitally important that all rail networks have strong and independent rail safety regulations.

Of even more terrifying significance today are terrorist threats to rail systems. For ten days in March 2004, SNCF rail maintenance staff joined police to search 35 000 kilometres of track right across France after a bomb was found with an intricate detonator and several plausible threats were received. And, of course, two hundred people were killed in the ten co-ordinated train bombings in Madrid in March 2004. Realistically, we should expect more bombings of rail targets. Security will therefore become a major focus for rail operators around the world.

Despite all this, rail is here to stay. Certainly there will be some spectacular financial collapses and sadly there will be accidents, but the renaissance of rail is set to continue into the 21st century. We will see China expand its networks, Europe and Japan lead the way in high-speed passenger train operation, Australia and the United States develop more efficient long-distance rail freight haulage, and South America celebrate multiple gauge operation. India, Russia and parts of South Africa all have enormous potential but need real political leadership for this potential to be fulfilled.

The Population Reference Bureau of the United Nations World Resources Institute has produced a fascinating set of statistics giving insight into the future of rail. Both the United States, the largest economy in the world, and China, the fastest growing economy, are of about the same size in terms of area. However, China with a population of 1 288 700 000, produces 2.5 tonnes of carbon dioxide emissions and consumes 880 kilograms oil equivalent per person per year. In the United States this figure is 19.8 tonnes of carbon dioxide at 7960 kilograms of oil per person per year. Per 1000 people, China has 16 cars and the United States 774 cars! Perversely, what this means is that both countries will have to expand their use of rail: China to quickly boost mass mobility and the United States as an alternative to gas guzzling cars and the finite opportunities for freeway expansion.

Today record numbers of people are travelling by train around the world. Freight services, including short line services in the United States, are doing well, indeed some are doing very well. In Australia, the Marulan south branch line is booming with limestone haulage, and short branch grain lines in New South Wales are currently carrying more freight than ever before, despite being threatened with closure.

Many mistakes have been made over the decades, but rail's underlying strength has ensured its survival and its expansion. If Los Angeles, of all places, can open a new suburban rail service (the Gold Line in 2003), and if Perth in Australia can commit to a new part underground suburban line, and if Chile can build a new fast electric rail passenger service from Santiago to Temuco and if overall passenger and rail freight haulage kilometres continue to climb, then surely there is hope for the future of rail. Even South Korea has opened a new high-speed railway from Seoul to Pusan.

As Robert Louis Stevenson once wrote: 'I travel not to go anywhere, but to go. I travel for travel's sake. The great affair is to move.' I travel to learn and to earn, to enjoy and be enthralled by the world and when I can I do so by train. I arrive a whole lot more relaxed and happier for the experience. We need rail now more than ever before for the joy of the experience, for the joy of seeing superb rail architecture, for the joy of being introduced to worlds that aren't necessarily our own.

The creator of Thomas the Tank Engine, the Reverend W. Awdry, once compared the Church of England and British railways:

Both had their heyday in the mid-nineteenth century, both own a good deal of Gothic-style architecture which is expensive to maintain, both are regularly assailed by critics, and both are convinced that they are the best means of getting man to his ultimate destination.

While I'm not qualified to comment on the Church of England, rail certainly hasn't passed its heyday. The great transcontinental railways in particular will help deliver us to our destinations on the planet earth. Try contacting the mighty Abraham, the great Buddha and Krishna for transport beyond.

BIBLIOGRAPHY

Adam-Smith, Patsy *Romance of Australian Railways* Melbourne, 1973, Rigby Ltd

Adam-Smith, Patsy *When We Rode the Rails* Melbourne, 1983, Cornstalk Publishing

Ambrose, Neil *Train Journeys of the World* London, 1993, AA Publishing

Amin, Mohamed *Railway Across the Equator* Nairobi, 1986, Camerapix Publishers

Balkwill, Richard *The Guinness Book of Railway Facts and Figures* London, 1971, Guinness Publishing

Bhandari, RR *Exotic Indian Mountain Railways* New Delhi, 1984, New Delhi Railways Ministry

Bright, Stephen *The Line Ahead* Brisbane, 1996, Catalyst Communication

Bryan, Tim *Brunel: the Great Engineer* Hersham UK, 1999, Ian Allan Publishing

Buchanan, Angus *Brunel* Bath UK, 2002, Hambledon & London

Burke, David *Road Through the Wilderness* Sydney, 1991, University of New South Wales

Churchman, Geoffrey *The Railways of New Zealand* Wellington NZ, 1990, HarperCollins

Cook, John *Australian Railway Journeys* Canberra, 1985, William Collins

DeBoer, David *Piggyback and Containers* San Marino USA, 1992, Golden West Books

Eastlake, Keith *Great Train Disasters* Sydney, 1997, Universal International

Ellis, Hamilton *Pictorial Encyclopedia of Railways* London, 1968, Hamlyn Publishing

Fearnside, GH *All Stations West* Sydney, 1970, Haldane Publishing

Fischler, Stan *Subways of the World* Osceola USA, 2000, MBI Publishing

Foxwell, Eric *Express Trains: English and Foreign*, London, 1889, Smith, Elder & Co

Garfield, Simon *The Last Journey of William Huskisson*, London, 2002, Faber & Faber

Gilbertson, Colin *Steam in Australia* Sydney, 1977, ARHS UNSW

Grigg, Arthur *Country Railway Men* Poole UK, 1985, Calypus Books

Gunn, John *The Defeat of Distance* Brisbane, 1985, University of Queensland Press

Harrigan, Leo *Victorian Railways to '62* Melbourne, 1962, Victorian Railways PBB

Harris, Ken *Jane's World Railways* Coulsdon UK, 2002, Bath Press

Holdsworth, Malcolm *Famous Last Lines* Sydney, 1993, Holdsworth Bambery Kingsford-Smith

Hollingsworth, Brian *North American Railways* Chicago, 1977, Summit

Hollingsworth, Brian *Atlas of the World's Railways* London, 1980, Rigby Ltd

Holmes, Lloyd *A Railway Life* Byron Bay, 1991, Holmes

Horsford, Jim *Barbados Railway* London, 2001, Paul Catchpole

Hosokawa, Bill *Old Man Thunder* Denver USA, 1997, Sogo Way

Jackson, David *A Guide to Trains* San Francisco, 2002, Fog City Press

Jay, Christopher *The Long Haul* Adelaide, 1991, Focus Books

Jordan, Peter *India: No Problems Sahib* Chesterfield, 1989, Three Counties Publishing

Keenan, David *Tramways of Sydney* Sydney, 1979, Transit Press

Kirk, John *The Forever Lands* Australia, 2001, Beyond Images

Laird, Philip *Back on Track* Sydney, 2001, UNSW

Lee, Robert *Colonial Engineer* Sydney, 2000, ARHS UNSW

Maggs, Colin *Rail Centres:Bristol* London, 1981, Ian Allen Ltd

McCormack, Gavan *The Burma Thailand Railway* Sydney, 1993, Allen & Unwin

Moustafine, Mara *Secrets and Spies: The Harbin Files*, Sydney, 2002, Random House

Newell, Brian *Following The Old Ghan* Adelaide, 2000, Custom Press

Nock, OS *World Atlas of Railways* London, 1978, Victoria House Publishing

Oakes, John *Sydney's Central* Sydney, 2002, ARHS UNSW

Oberg, Leon *Australian Rail at Work* Australia, 1995, Kangaroo Press

Patterson, JH *The Man-Eaters of Tvaso* London, 1907, MacMillan

Portway, Christopher *The World Commuter* Chichester 2001, Summersdale Publishers

Reid, Arnot *From Peking to Petersburg* London, 1899, Edward Arnold

Robbins, Michael *The Railway Age* London, 1962, Manchester University

Roberts, Lew *Rails to Wealth* Broken Hill 1995, L E Roberts

Rowe, Trevor *Narrow Guage Railways of Spain,* Vol 1&2, Horley UK, 1995, Plateway Press

Rowe, Trevor *The Railways of South America* London, 2000, Paul Catchpole

Rozendall, Jack *Steam & Rail in Indonesia* London, 2000, Paul Catchpole

Sallis, Roger *Australian Preservation of Narrow Gauge* Adelaide, 1979, Peacock Publications

Sallis, Roger *Railways in the Adelaide Hills* Adelaide, 1998, Open Book Publishers

Scafer, Mike *Classic American Railroads* Osceola USA, 1996, MBI Publishing

Seidenfaden, Eric *Bangkok Siam Railway Guide* Bangkok, 1928, Royal State Railways Siam

Semmens, Peter *High Speed in Japan* Sheffield UK, 1997, Semmens & Platform 5

Sharma, SN *History of the Great Indian Peninsula Railways* Bombay, 1990, Central Railway Bombay

Sheppard, Charles *Railway Stations* London, 1996, Universal International

Simmons, Jack *The Railways of Britain* London, 1990, Mallard Press

Singleton, CC *Railways of Australia* Sydney, 1963, Angus & Robertson

Smith, Keith *Tales from a Railway Odyssey* Adelaide, 2001, Railmac Publications

Stover, John *The Routledge Atlas of American Railways* London, 1999, Routledge

Stringer, H *China: A New Aspect* London, 1929, HF & G Witherby

Talbot, Frederick *Railway Wonders of the World* London, 1920, Cassell & Company

Tayler, Arthur *High Tech Trains* London, 1992, New Birlington Books

Taylor, Colin *Train Catcher* Sydney, 1996, IPL Publishing

Welsh, Joe *The American Railroad* Osceola USA, 1999, MBI Publishing

Westwood, John *World Railways* London, 2001, PRC Publishing

Wheaton, Timothy *Luxury Trains* London, 1995, Bison Books

Wood, Heather *Third-Class Ticket* London, 1980, Routledge & Kegan Paul

GLOSSARY OF RAILWAY TERMINOLOGY

Herewith is an explanation of some of the key terms and phrases used in the construction and operation of railways over the decades. You will note it is in reverse alphabetical order. I do this for three reasons. First, the more colourful and interesting terms are towards the far end of the alphabet and need elevating. Second, to counter-balance the order of the index. This is a gesture in salute to the 200th anniversary of reciprocating steam piston motion. I have forgotten the third reason. This is in celebration of Mark Twain's comments, made over a century ago when he was forced to change trains in Albury Station because of break of gauge. Please enjoy this glossary.

Zig zag: Used by railway engineers to rapidly gain or lose height by providing for a train to cross points into a loop. The points are then switched and the train changes direction and reverses out of the loop, to continue its climb or descent. Often used in mountainous areas. The best example is on the Khyber Pass in Pakistan.

Y points: A set of points laid out so that the centre line of the single section of track is different to but equidistant to the centre line of each of the double tracks.

XPT: The generic term used for passenger trains in New South Wales that are usually, but not always, configured as locomotive, carriages, locomotive. The XPT was based on the high-speed train sets of Great Britain.

Whistle stop: Generally a tiny country station where trains stop very briefly, for the duration of one whistle blast.

VFT: The term applied to the Melbourne–Canberra–Sydney high speed train project developed by Dr Paul Wild in the 1980s. Loosely patterned on the French TGV, it was killed off by deeply negative elements in the then federal government.

Uniform loading specifications: Different national rail systems, for example in Europe, may well have the same rail gauge width between rails but different loading requirements for both size above rail and weight. Uniform loading specifications provide harmonised standards.

TGV: The French TGV (*Train à Grande Vitesse*) has held the world speed record of 526 kph for many years. This all electric train has a near perfect safety record.

Steam locomotive: Took over from the horse as the main method of haulage in the first half of the 19th century. Many steam locomotives have names that have become legend over the centuries, including The Rocket, Mallard, Thomas Mitchell and 3801.

Rail track: The term applying to the two steel rails, sleeper or tie, clip or spike, pad and ballast. Today the head of each rail line is cantered in by about 1 in 20.

Quagmire: Also called mud hole, this is a short section of track where the ballast has turned to powder or been washed away causing sleepers to drop down, thus creating an uneven ride which, if not fixed, can lead to derailments. Quagmires can occur along tracks in desert locations and during drought.

Pacific class: The arrangement of steam locomotive wheels on the basis of four small, then six large and then two supporting wheels, as opposed to all other combinations.

Oscillation: Also called hunting, this term describes lateral movement or sideway movement in carriages and wagons due to a mismatch of wheel profile on railhead profile, or when the rail track is badly maintained and the gauge width actually varies by up to one half of one inch.

Near miss: An aviation term that also refers to trains being cleared onto the same pathway or track but not colliding. This can be in the same direction or worse still, in the opposing direction, risking a head on crash.

Motion sickness: More common in sea and air travel, but also experienced by train passengers, particularly when travelling on rough riding trains on old tracks.

Loading gauge: The maximum height and width above rail that carriages, wagons and/or containers can occupy. In Europe this is known as Berne gauge. India and the United States have the biggest loading gauges in the world while Great Britain has one of the smallest even though its systems operate on standard gauge.

Kitchenette : Not many are left on trains today, but the dining cars of the Blue Train, the Orient Express, the Indian Pacific and The Ghan all have stainless steel kitchens producing gourmet meals from cramped quarters. There is a certain joy conferred by eating a meal on board that has actually been cooked on board.

Jump track: This occurs when rail wheels jump the track and derail, but the train remains vertical. This generally happens only when the derailment is at slow speed and on relatively straight track.

Inching forward: The process of coupling wagons, carriages and locomotives together under power.

Hump marshalling yard: Used in large freight yards. Wagons are pushed up a hump and then released though a set of computer controlled braking pads and several sets of points at just the right speed to hook onto wagons already there.

Gauge: Simply the distance between the inside of each rail at their nearest point.

Frame: Used in mechanical signal control boxes. A steel frame below the points and signal control levers prevents false moves being made thus ensuring trains are not put on a collision path.

Express: This should denote passenger and freight trains that run without stopping, other than at major stations, from starting point to end destination. It is an overused term in some railway systems.

Departure: In freight terminology this means when a freight train has been assembled and checked and has cleared the freight terminal onto the main line. For passenger trains, it is the moment the train moves away from the platform. The time of departure has become more important as today penalties often attach to delays.

Coupling: Today almost all couplings are heavy, semi-automatic steel jaws and clasps, designed to absorb jolting and prevent too much stretch. They are a far cry from the original hook and ring type.

Bogie: The set of rail wheels, axles and frame with central pin attaching to the wagon/carriage or locomotive. At some break of gauge borders, trains are jacked up and bogies changed.

Arrival: Now a hotly disputed term. It is the moment a passenger train stops moving having reached the designated platform. However, some railway systems have a 5 minute period of grace in defining on time arrival; others allow 10 minutes. With efficient freight train operations today, it is often the case that the first containers are coming off a train within 30 seconds of arrival at the freight terminal or siding.

ACKNOWLEDGEMENTS

It has been a long and interesting journey writing this book, but I was greatly helped by the support of my wife and family. Their tolerance of my rail research escapades, the spread of rail material throughout the house has been terrific and beyond what I should expect.

To the Allen & Unwin team and the late John Iremonger, who launched me down a book-writing path, my sincere thanks. My thanks in particular to editor/publisher Rebecca Kaiser, nicknamed Kaiser Wilhelm the Third, who has maintained constant faith in the book.

I happily declare my thanks to FreightLink for the ride on the first freight train from Adelaide to Darwin and to Great Southern Railway for the ride on the legendary Ghan, in part as South Australian government envoy to the Rail to Asia project.

Sam Burgess of Zig Zag fame, Donald Hawes of Springwood and Mike Mohan of Perth and the USA deserve my thanks for their reviews and help pre-editing, as do Annette Doherty and Glenda Jones in preparing the manuscript.

I acknowledge with thanks AAP, GRMS, GSR, News Limited and Rail Digest for direct and indirect help with the photo section. Particular thanks goes to Thomas Roschi, Jonathan Thomas, John Fuhrman, John Kirk and John Phillips.

Over the years I have been guided on rail policy and rail operations by several great thinkers including Dr Fred Affleck, John Anderson, Stephen Bradford, Dale Budd, Milton Morris, Vince O'Rourke and John Sharp. My thanks to them and the many others who have contributed ideas and information.

Special thanks goes to those who helped with the research for the related gauge posters, including Dmitry Zinoviev, John Birchmeier, Alex Grubac, Owen Johnstone-Donnet, Dr Rob Lee, Scott Martin and Gerry Willis. Posters of the great Australian railway gauges and the great world railway gauges are available through famu@bigpond.com with proceeds going to rail heritage projects.

Part of the royalties from this book will be donated to the Fred Hollows Foundation, the Frontier Services (formerly the Inland Mission of Flynn of the Inland), the Royal Flying Doctor Service of Australia and the South Australian government.

It has been fun, and a long haul but I hope one you the reader, enjoys.

INDEX